Revitalizing Agricultural Soils in Mehsana and Narmada Districts: Bio-Rejuvenation Studies

Anand Row

Copyright © [2023]

Author: Anand Row

Title: Revitalizing Agricultural Soils in Mehsana and Narmada Districts: Bio Rejuvenation Studies

All rights reserved. No part of this book may be reproduced or transmitted in any form or by any means, electronic or mechanical, including photocopying, recording, or by any information storage and retrieval system, without permission in writing from the author.

This book is a product of

ISBN:

CONTENTS

Title	Page no.
Chapter 1 Introduction	1-14
Chapter 2 Review of Literature	15-30
Chapter 3 Materials and Methods	31-81
Chapter 4 Result and Discussion	82-134
Chapter 5 Summary and Conclusion	135-139

List of Tables

Table No.	Table Title	Page No
Table-2.1	Essential Plant Nutrient Elements and their primary form utilized by Plants	19
Table-2.2	Bacterial Culturability among Various Habitats	25
Table-3.1	Terms used in Colonial Morphology	70
Table-4.1	Soil Moisture Analysis of Mehsana District	82-83
Table-4.2	Soil Moisture Analysis of Narmada District	83
Table-4.3	Soil Bulk Density Analysis of Mehsana District	84-85
Table-4.4	Soil Bulk Density Analysis of Narmada District	85
Table-4.5	Soil Texture Analysis of Mehsana District	86-87
Table-4.6	Soil Texture Analysis of Narmada District	87
Table-4.7	Soil pH Analysis of Mehsana District	89
Table-4.8	Soil pH Analysis of Narmada District	89
Table-4.9	Soil Electrical Conductivity Analysis of Mehsana District	90
Table-4.10	Soil Electrical Conductivity Analysis of Narmada District	90-91
Table-4.11	Soil Organic Carbon Analysis of Mehsana District	92
Table-4.12	Soil Organic Carbon Analysis of Narmada District	92
Table-4.13	Soil Nitrogen Analysis of Mehsana District	93-94
Table-4.14	Soil Nitrogen Analysis of Narmada District	94
Table-4.15	Soil Phosphorous Analysis of Mehsana District	95-96
Table-4.16	Soil Phosphorous Analysis of Narmada	96

	District	
Table-4.17	Soil Potassium Analysis of Mehsana District	97
Table-4.18	Soil Potassium Analysis of Narmada District	97-98
Table-4.19	Soil Zink Analysis of Mehsana District	99
Table-4.20	Soil Zink Analysis of Narmada District	99
Table-4.21	Soil Copper Analysis of Mehsana District	100-101
Table-4.22	Soil Copper Analysis of Narmada District	101
Table-4.23	Soil Iron Analysis of Mehsana District	102
Table-4.24	Soil Iron Analysis of Narmada District	102-103
Table-4.25	Soil Manganese Analysis of Mehsana District	103-104
Table-4.26	Soil Manganese Analysis of Narmada District	104
Table-4.27	Soil Colony Forming Units Analysis of Mehsana District	105
Table-4.28	Soil Colony Forming Units Analysis of Narmada District	105-106
Table-4.29	Descriptive Statistics for the Mehsana District	107
Table-4.30	One-Sample Test for the Mehsana District	108
Table-4.31	Correlation table for Mehsana District	111
Table-4.32	Descriptive Statistics for the Narmada District	112
Table-4.33	One-Sample Test for the Narmada District	113
Table-4.34	Correlation table for Narmada District	115
Table-4.35	Independent Sample Test (T-test) for both the District	117
Table-4.36	Cultural Characteristics of Bacterial Isolates	118

Table-4.37	Biochemical Characteristics of Bacterial Isolates	119
Table-4.38	Soil Analyses of the Selected Agricultural Fields	130
Table-4.39	Soil Analyzed Result after the Amendment of Bacterial Isolates	130
Table-4.40	Effect of Amendment on Crop fields of both the Districts	134

List of Figures

Table No.	Figure Title	Page No
Fig.-1.1	Soil Map of Gujarat State	3
Fig.-1.2	Land Use Land Cover of the Gujarat State	7
Fig.-2.1	Three Domain of Life	28
Fig.-3.1	Mehsana District Land Use Land Cover	32
Fig.-3.2	Narmada District Land Use Land Cover	34
Fig.-3.3	Q-GIS based Random Soil Sampling for Mehsana District	35
Fig.-3.4	Google Earth Image for Random Soil Sampling of Mehsana District	35
Fig.-3.5	Q-GIS based Random Soil Sampling for Narmada District	36
Fig.-3.6	Google Earth Image for Random Soil Sampling of Narmada District	36
Fig.-3.7	Collection of Soil Sample	37
Fig.-3.8	Air drying of Soil Sample	37
Fig.-3.9	Soil Moisture Content Dish	38
Fig.-3.10	Soil Bulk Density Testing	39
Fig.-3.11	Soil Texture Triangle	41
Fig.-3.12	pH Meter	43
Fig.-3.13	Soil Electrical Conductivity Testing	44
Fig.-3.14	Soil Organic Carbon Testing	46
Fig.-3.15	Kjeldahl Nitrogen Determination Method	47
Fig.-3.16	Flame Photometer	52
Fig.-3.17	Atomic Absorption Spectrometer	54
Fig.-3.18	Colony Forming Unit count on Colony Counter	60
Fig.-3.19	Preparation of Nutrient Agar Plates	62
Fig.-3.20	Preparation of Serial Dilution	63

Fig.-3.21	The Hanging Drop Slide of Motility Test	68
Fig.-4.1	Gram Negative NFB	119
Fig.-4.2	Gram Positive PSB	119
Fig.-4.3	Gram Negative KSB	119
Fig.-4.4	Representation of sequenced *Azotobacter sp.* strain DPN (GenBank Accession Number MT656171)	121
Fig.-4.5	Representation of sequenced *Bacillus sp.* strain DPP (GenBank Accession Number MT656254)	121
Fig.-4.6	Output result of BLAST performed for *Azotobacter sp.* Strain DPN	122
Fig.-4.7	Output result of BLAST performed for *Azotobacter sp.* Strain DPN (page-1)	123
Fig.-4.8	Output result of BLAST performed for *Bacillus sp.* Strain DPP	124
Fig.-4.9	Output result of BLAST performed for *Bacillus sp.* Strain DPP (page-1)	125
Fig.-4.10	GeneBank entry of *Azotobacter sp.* Strain DPN	126
Fig.-4.11	GeneBank entry of *Bacillus sp.* Strain DPP	127
Fig.-4.12	Phylogenetic Tree Representing the Position of *Azotobacter sp.* Strain DPN	128
Fig.-4.13	Phylogenetic Tree Representing the Position of *Bacillus sp.* Strain DPP	128
Fig.-4.14	Bacterial Isolates Mixed with Carrier for Amendment	131
Fig.-4.15	Castor field 1 Mehsana District	131
Fig.-4.16	Castor field 2 Mehsana District	131
Fig.-4.17	Sugarcane field Narmada District	131
Fig.-4.18	Sugarcane field Narmada District	131

List of Graphs

Table No.	Graph Title	Page No
Graph-4.1	Mehsana District soil Moisture	84
Graph-4.2	Narmada District soil Moisture	84
Graph-4.3	Mehsana District soil BD	84
Graph-4.4	Narmada District soil BD	84
Graph-4.5	Mehsana District soil Texture	88
Graph-4.6	Narmada District soil Texture	88
Graph-4.7	Mehsana District soil pH	88
Graph-4.8	Narmada District soil pH	88
Graph-4.9	Mehsana District soil EC	91
Graph-4.10	Narmada District soil EC	91
Graph-4.11	Mehsana District soil OC	93
Graph-4.12	Narmada District soil OC	93
Graph-4.13	Mehsana District soil N	94
Graph-4.14	Narmada District soil N	94
Graph-4.15	Mehsana District soil P	95
Graph-4.16	Narmada District soil P	95
Graph-4.17	Mehsana District soil K	98
Graph-4.18	Narmada District soil K	98
Graph-4.19	Mehsana District soil Zn	100
Graph-4.20	Narmada District soil Zn	100
Graph-4.21	Mehsana District soil Cu	101
Graph-4.22	Narmada District soil Cu	101
Graph-4.23	Mehsana District soil Fe	103
Graph-4.24	Narmada District soil Fe	103
Graph-4.25	Mehsana District soil Mn	104
Graph-4.26	Narmada District soil Mn	104
Graph-4.27	Mehsana District soil CFUs	106
Graph-4.28	Narmada District soil CFUs	106

Graph-4.29	Comparison of OC% in Selected Fields after Amendment	132
Graph-4.30	Comparison of N% in Selected Fields after Amendment	132
Graph-4.31	Comparison of P (ppm) in Selected Fields after Amendment	133
Graph-4.32	Comparison of K (ppm) in Selected Fields after Amendment	133

Chapter 1
Introduction

Introduction

1.0 Introduction

India is an agricultural practice-driven country, so the soil is of extraordinary worth. Soil is one of the significant assets for a living. Loose rock minerals together with humus that structure the upper loosely composed layer of the earth is called soil. Soil and land is an integral part of the ecosystem, is the most important gift for the survival of humanity. Man for ages has been linked with the use and maltreatment of soil, an inelastic component of the ecosystem, with the results being prosperity or ruin of civilizations. Soil is a crucial life-supporting natural resource since it produces food that is the basis of man's existence. Soil information is a slow process; it is a dynamic, living, natural body that is vital to the function of terrestrial ecosystems and represents a unique balance between physical, chemical, and biological factors.

1.1. Soil and Its Importance

The soil may be defined as the weathered superficial layer of the earth's crust which mingled with living organisms and products of their decay. Typically, the soil is made up of parent material (the inorganic foundation or mineral networks) into which there has been incorporated an organic increment as well as living organisms, with the space remaining between the solid particles filled with water and gases. Soil is an important factor that influences the productivity of our planet's various ecosystems. Soil is vital for the existence of every form of life that has evolved on this planet. For example, soil provides vascular plants with a medium for growth and supplies these organisms with most of their nutritional requirements. Further, the nutrient status of the ecosystem's soil not only limits both plant growth, but also the productivity of consumer-type organisms that are further down the food chain. The soil itself is very complex. It would be exceptionally off-base to consider soil only an assortment of fine mineral particles. Soil also contains air, water, dead organic matter, and various types of living organisms. The development of soil is impacted by organisms, climate, topography, parent material, and time.

Soil is supplying virtually 5 F's Viz., forest, fuel, food, fodder, and fiber that sustain the human population and providing ecosystem services that support life;

Introduction

these are non-renewable natural resources in the human lifetime frame (Lal, 2009). Physical deterioration of soil involves the destruction of soil structure, dispersion of soil particles, sealing of pores, compression, and increasing density, consolidation, compaction, and reduced root penetration, low infiltration, waterlogging and runoff, and accelerated erosion (Greene, 2005). Soil erosion involves mainly two processes detachment of particles from soil aggregates and transportation of the particles by water or wind (Meena, 2013). Nutrient depletion has caused serious nutrient imbalances in all soils under low-input agriculture in marginal lands. In many studies, all the world agricultural soils exhibited negative NPK (nitrogen, phosphorus, potassium) balances. Nutrient exhaustion is caused by leaching, residue harvest and burning, erosion, and crop removal. The new alternatives ought to be productive and cost-effective, but furthermore must be particularly sustainable in terms of agricultural production and food security (Meena *et al.*, 2014). Worldwide, conservation agriculture plays a major role in improving soil ecology. To achieve self-sufficiency in food, fiber and edible oil for efficient use of natural resources, solar radiation, precipitation, and conservation agriculture is a management system that maintains a soil cover through surface retention of crop residues. The soil may be defined as the weathered superficial layer of the earth's crust which mingled with living organisms and products of their decay.

1.2. Major Soil types in Gujarat State

The state is enriched with a wide range of macro and microclimates, physiography, landforms, geology, and vegetation that affect the genesis of soil. Soil systems have developed over many millions of years. The soil qualities in a given region at a given purpose of time are an element of both regular impacts and human exercises. The soil of Gujarat is broadly classified into 9 major groups (Fig.-1.1). There are black soil, mixed red and black soil, residual sandy soil, alluvial soil, saline/alkali soil, lateritic soil, hilly soil, desert soil, and forest soil (Biswas *et al.*, 1985).

1.2.1. Black Soil: Black Soil is the most dominant soil type of Gujarat. There are three types of Black Soil, namely (i) shallow black soil, (ii) medium black soil, and (iii) deep black soil.

Introduction

1.2.1.1. The shallow black soil: The shallow black soil is developed from the basaltic trap in the Saurashtra region. This soil is mainly sandy clay loam in nature and poor infertility. Deccan trap in the extreme eastern part and the remaining strips in Chhotaudepur and Saurashtra districts have developed from granite and gneiss parent material. So there is a light gray color. In some places soil is gravelly but mainly it is sandy clay loam in texture.

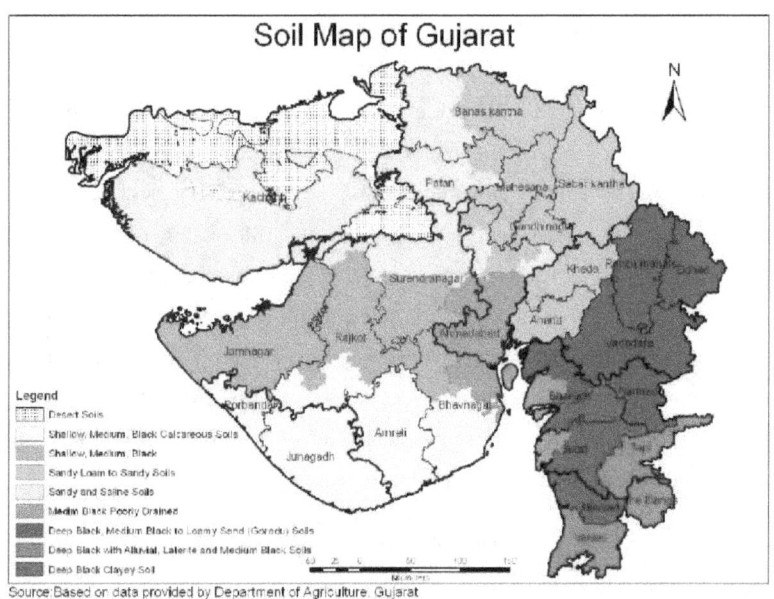

Fig.-1.1: Soil Map of Gujarat State

1.2.1.2. The medium black soils: It is residual soil having basaltic trap parent material. That is found largely in Sabarkantha and Panchmahal districts, developed from the granite and gneiss parent material. It is calcareous, and a layer of murrain (unconsolidated material of decomposed trap and limestone) is found below a depth of about 40 cm, especially in the Saurashtra region. The color of these soil varies from dark grey to light grey, are silty loam to clay in texture, with neutral to alkaline in reaction.

1.2.1.3. The deep black soil: This soil has its origin in the trap. It is dominating the districts of Bhavnagar, Surat, Valsad, and South Vadodra. The depth varies from 60 cm to as high as a few meters. The tract of '*Bhal*' comprising of the area between Dhandhuka and Bhavnagar has typical deep black soil formed due to decomposition of trap parent material transported through the flow of rivers radiating from the plateau of Central Saurashtra. The '*Ghed*' tract of Junagadh district covering mainly talukas of Porebander, Kutiyana, Manavadar, and part of Mangrol have deep black soil formed due to deposition of basaltic trap material transported by rivers. This soil is also impregnated with quite a high amount of free line. The soil is dark brown to very dark grayish brown, containing 40-70 percent clay, is poor in drainage, and neutral to the alkaline reaction. This soil is more fertile than other black soil.

1.2.2. Red and Black Soil: This soil is shallow in depth with reddish-brown color at higher elevations and grayish brown at lower elevations. This is clay loam to clay and skeletal, with up to 50 percent stony material in the subsurface layer, providing ideal drainage conditions to this soil. Mix red and black soil are highly calcareous in nature and alkaline in reaction.

1.2.3. Residual Sandy Soil: This soil has developed in situ from the parent material originated from red sandstone and shale. This residual soil is shallow in depth, reddish-brown in color with fine weak granular structure, sandy to loamy sand in texture dominated by coarse sand. They are non-calcareous, neutral to alkaline in reaction with poor base saturation. In the Kutch district, they are affected due to salt accumulation. This soil is also fertile.

1.2.4. Alluvial Soil: This soil has been formed due to silting by the Indus river system. This soil is very deep, coarse sandy, and is found in Banaskantha and part of Mehsana due to the deposition of coarse material from flowing rivers. The alluvial sandy loam to sandy clay loam cover, the entire northern districts of Banaskantha, Mehsana, and bordering Sabarkantha. This is non-calcareous, neutral to alkaline in reaction. The alluvial sandy loam to sandy clay loam soil is found in Kheda and Gandhinagar districts, the eastern part of Ahmedabad district, the southern part of Mehsana, and the western part of Vadodra district. The coastal alluvial soil is sandy clay loam to clay in texture, neutral to highly alkaline in reaction, and has medium fertility.

1.2.5. Laterite: In the Dangs district, due to abundant forest vegetation and high annual rainfall laterite is developed. It is yellowish red on the upper horizon, with thickness ranging from 20-40 cm. This is neutral to slightly acidic in reaction.

1.2.6. Hill Soil: This soil occurs in the hilly areas of Surendranagar, Amreli, Jamnagar, Bhavnagar, and Junagadh districts of Saurashtra, Kutch, and the eastern strip of mainland Gujarat. It is shallow in depth, composed of undecomposed rock fragments, and is poor infertility.

1.2.7. Desert Soil: The two ranns (deserts) of Kutch, viz. little runn and greater runn, have these soil formed as a result of the geological process of Pleistocene age in Indogangetic depression. It is fairly deep; light gray, sandy to sandy loam, with silty clay loam texture in some areas. The salt content is very high with NaCl (Sodium Chloride) as the dominant salt in the soil.

1.2.8. Forest Soil: The soil of the Junagadh forest contains more sand and is neutral. The soil of Dangs forest has a higher silt fraction and is acidic. Organic matter and lime contents are high in Junagadh soil compared to Dang's soil.

1.2.9. Saline Soil: The majority of Salt-affected soil groups are found in the state. The major areas affected are due to the desert soils in Kutch and those affected along the sea coast due to the ingress of seawater. The Bhal tract is the area with flat topography formed due to the Alluvial deposits brought by the rivers like Narmada, Mahi, Sabarmati, and Bhogavo flowing into the Gulf of Cambay. The rivers Bhadar, Ozat, Minsar, Madhuvanti, etc. have formed a delta which is known as Ghed. Waterlogging for a long time has created saline conditions.

1.3.   Land Use Land Cover of the Gujarat State

Land is the most important natural resource on which all activities are based. Land-use unlike geology is dynamic and is indeed changing. The increase in population and human activities are increasing the demand on the limited land and soil resources for agriculture, forest, pasture, urban and industrial land uses. India is facing a serious problem of natural resource scarcity, especially that of water because of population growth and economic development (Yadav *et al.*, 2013). Land Use Land Cover (LULC) changes are affected by human intervention and natural

Introduction

phenomena such as agricultural demand and trade, population growth and consumption patterns, urbanization and economic development, science and technology, and other factors. LULC change has become a subject of colossal enthusiasm inside the human components of the environmental change research community (Meyer and Turner, 1996). As a result, information about LULC is essential for any kind of natural resource management and action planning. Convenient and precise information about LULC change detection of the earth's surface is extremely important for understanding relationships and interactions between human and natural phenomena for better management of decision making (Lu et al., 2004). There is a proceeding with interest for precise and up-to-date LULC information for any kind of sustainable development program where LULC serves as one of the major input criteria. Human alterations of the terrestrial surface of the earth are unprecedented in their pace, magnitude, and spatial reach, of these, none are more important than changes in land cover and land use (Turner et al., 1994). Though land-use changes are an indirect consequence of national economic growth, it is important to evaluate land-use changes in the regional and the local context to assist in anticipating the impacts associated with change and contributes to an understanding of productive environmental sustainability (Laymon, 2003).

LULC for the Gujarat state, as per the Bhuvan: ISRO/NRSC, 2019 information which has appeared in Fig.-1.2. The total geographical area of the state is 196024 sq. km. Agricultural cropland covers more than 50 percent of the total state land. Total urban, rural and mining buildup land occupy 2.84 percent. Forest and grassland are altogether 6.71 percent of the state LULC, among these 9191.95 sq. km. covers the deciduous forest. 42269.5 sq. km. of land is barren, uncultivable, wetlands. And more than 6 percent of land covers the waterbody of the state which incorporates inland wetland, coastal wetland, river, stream, canals, reservoir, ponds, and lakes.

Introduction

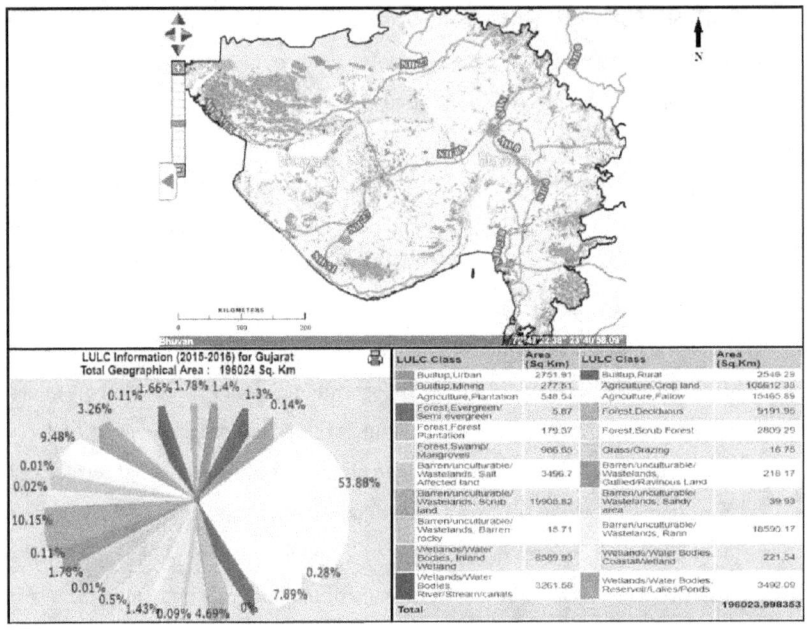

(*Source* - Bhuvan: ISRO/NRSC, 2019)

Fig.-1.2: Land Use Land Cover of the Gujarat State

1.4. Agricultural Importance in Indian Economy

The economy of India flourishes with agriculture; the most labor-intensive occupation and assumes an imperative role in the nation. It has advanced since the beginning of human development, first as a means to guarantee food supply, and then, as a wellspring of family income and improved profitability (Gasser and Fraley, 1989). The direct contribution of the agriculture sector to the national economy is reflected by its share in total Gross Domestic Product (GDP). Agriculture is a significant part of the Indian economy as it and unified divisions like forestry and fishing represented 18.5 percent of absolute Indian GDP in 2005-06 (at 1999-2000 consistent costs) and employed about 58 percent of the country's workforce (CSO, 2007). It accounted for 10.95 percent of India's exports in 2005-06 (GoI, 2007) and about 46 percent of India's geographical area is used for agricultural activity. Indian agriculture has registered impressive growth over the last few decades. The food grains yield has expanded from 51 million tons in 1950-51 to 250 million tons during

Introduction

2011-12 most noteworthy since the independence. So, the health of agricultural soil has always been important for farmers to get more yields.

There has been a structural transformation in the Indian economy during the past few decades. The composition of GDP at 1993-94 constant prices reveals that the share of agriculture including forestry and fishing has declined as growth in industrial and services sectors far outpaced the agricultural sector. Despite a steady decline of its share in the GDP, agriculture is as yet significant and plays a significant role in the overall socio-economic development of the country. Therefore, fostering rapid, sustained, and broad-based growth in agriculture remains a key priority for the government. Despite the declining share of agriculture in the economy, the majority of the workforce continues to depend on the agricultural sector for employment, and in rural areas depend on agriculture is more as nearly 75 percent of the rural population is employed in the agricultural sector. Agriculture in India is unavoidably the obligation of the states rather than the central government. The central government's role is in formulating policy and providing financial resources for agriculture to the states.

1.5. Soil Profile and Factor Affecting Soil Development

The weathered parent material of the soil, may not have time to attain the state of equilibrium which characterized maturity, is made up of a series of superimposed layers or horizon. Each of them was affected differently by the weathering processes, and which collectively are referred to as the soil profile. The various horizons in a profile may differ in color, structure, consistency, thickness reaction, and chemical composition. Under a particular type of climatic influence, all parent materials of the soil tend toward the same general type of profile. However, the details of the mature soil profile are determined by the type of vegetation that grew on the soil, the physiographic processes of erosion or deposition drainage, and the nature of the original parent materials.

1.5.1. Effects of Climate on Soil Development

The bioclimatic regions of the earth's surface will in general be organized in a zonal grouping which is represented basically by the pole-equator temperature

Introduction

gradient. Therefore each takes the form of a circumpolar belt by occupying a particular range of latitude. Mountain region producing aridity and that influences the other systems of zones which governed more by aridity than by temperature and more consequently centered about the mountains. In the abundant rainfall climate, precipitation exceeds evaporation and transpiration, the excess rainwater sinks through the soil and escapes from the area as streams. Here, the net movement of soil water is downward, certain soluble nutrients are continually lost and frequently the soil is developing. In such conditions, the temperature is the most important climatic variable.

1.5.2. Effects of Vegetation on Soil Development

It is difficult to draw a clear distinction between the impacts of climate and vegetation upon the nature of the soil profile for microclimate, vegetation, and soil. At the point when one factor from this complex has adjusted the others similarly change and a new equilibrium is established. Grassland profiles tend to develop in forest climates. Wherever the forest is kept cleared away so that herbaceous vegetation remains in control of the soil. Also, when a forest is cleared and replaced with grain fields, the organic matter may increase as the result of crop residues, despite the usual tendency for cultivation to decrease humus. Then again, grassland soils develop some of the characteristics of a forest soil profile. The impact of various forest types upon the soil is distinct in that the substitution of one forest type by another produces surprising changes in the profile within a couple of decades. The changes from one vegetation type to another bring changes in microclimate and in the chemical nature of the organic increment which the plants add to the soil. The vegetation exerts a strong influence on soil development because no two different vegetation types produce the same microclimate at the level of the soil. Though, they do not produce the same kind of organic matter. The truth of the matter is various types of plants have different effects on soil properties. It is of great practical importance in forestry. However, in agricultural applications, soil fertility is maintained by the addition of fertilizer. Besides, a significant point of yield revolution is the improvement of the soil.

Introduction

1.6. The Function of Soil Biota

There is an intense need to conserve biodiversity at the worldwide level to preserve the endemic and endangered species, both microscopic and macroscopic which play a vital role in the maintenance of the sustainable environment, agriculture, and forestry (Jha *et al.*, 2002). The functions of soil biota are central to deterioration procedures and nutrient cycling. Microbial diversity plays a dominant role in the maintenance of the ecosystem. Soil microorganisms are the major organisms responsible for controlling the amount of nutrient cycling and for controlling the number of nutrients available to plants (Hernot and Robertson, 1994; Singh and Rai, 2004; Jain *et al.*, 2005). Soil fungi also one of the important microbe to make a significant piece of the environment alongside different microorganisms in the turnover of the biomass (James and Hyde, 1998). The soil microbes decompose the plant and animal residues and convert them into soil organic matter, which impacts soil physical, chemical, and biological properties and on creating a complementary medium for biological reactions and life support in the soil environment (Olson *et al.*, 2000). Soil fertility status is reliant upon soil microbial components and their mediated processes (Lynch, 1984).

1.6.1. Soil Bacteria and Its Characteristics

Bacteria are some of the smallest and most rich organisms in the soil. In a solitary gram of soil, there can be billions of bacteria. It is estimated that 60000 different bacteria species, a large portion of which still can't seem to be even named, and everyone has its specific roles and abilities. Most live in the top 10 cm of soil where organic matter is present. Some bacteria species are very delicate and can be destroyed by slight changes in the soil condition. Other species are amazingly intense, able to withstand severe heat, cold, or drying. Some can lie dormant for decades waiting for favorable conditions. Others can extricate nitrogen straightforwardly from the air or separate some harmful substances. Populations of microbes can boom or go bust in the space of a few days in response to changes in soil moisture, soil temperature, or carbon substrate. To increase a preferred position in this procedure, many microbes release antibiotic substances to suppress particular competitors. Along these lines, a few species can stifle other disease-causing microorganisms. Here, some of the main types of bacteria are discussed below:

a. Decomposers: Bacteria play an important role in the decomposition of organic materials, especially in the early stages of decomposition when moisture levels are high; in the later stages fungi tend to dominate. *Bacillus subtilis* and *Pseudomonas fluorescens* are examples of decomposer bacteria. Additions of these bacteria have not been proved to accelerate the formation of compost or humus in the soil.

b. Nitrogen Fixers: *Rhizobium* bacteria can be inoculated onto legume seeds to fix nitrogen from the air and convert it into forms that plants can use from the soil. These nitrogen-fixing bacteria live in special root nodules on legumes such as clover, beans, wattles, etc. This form of nitrogen fixation can add the equivalent of more than 100 kg of nitrogen per hectare per year. *Azotobacter, Azospirillum, Agrobacterium, Gluconobacter, Flavobacterium,* and *Herbaspirillum* are all examples of free-living, nitrogen-fixing bacteria, often associated with legumes. To date, inoculating the soil with these organisms has not proved an effective means of increasing nitrogen fixation for non-legume crops.

c. Disease Suppressors: *Bacillus megaterium, Pseudomonas fluorescens* are an example of bacterium those have been used on some crops to suppress the disease-causing fungus *Rhizoctonia solani*. *Bacillus subtilis* has been used to suppress seedling blight of sunflowers, caused by *Alternaria helianthi* (Plant-Pathogen). Several bacteria have been commercialized worldwide for disease suppression. However, suppression is often specific to particular diseases of particular crops and may only be effective in certain circumstances.

d. Aerobes and Anaerobes: Aerobic bacteria are those that need oxygen, so where the soil is well-drained aerobes tend to dominate. Anaerobes are bacteria that do not need oxygen and may find them toxic. This group includes very ancient types of bacteria that live inside soil aggregates. Anaerobic bacteria favor wet, poorly drained soils and can produce toxic compounds that can limit root growth and predispose plants to root diseases.

e. Actinobacteria: These soil bacteria help to slowly break down humates and humic acids in soils. Actinobacteria prefer non-acidic soils with a pH higher than 5.

Introduction

f. Sulfur Oxidizers: Many soil minerals contain sulfides which are largely unavailable to plants. *Thiobacillus* bacteria can covert sulfides into sulfates, a form of sulfur that plants can use.

1.6.2. Other Soil Microorganisms

Possible other soil microorganisms which live in the soil other than bacteria are discussed below (Tugel and Lewandowski, 2010):

a. Soil Algae: Soil algae (both prokaryotes and eukaryotes) grow where an adequate amount of moisture and sunlight are present. They are very important for soil. One of the important roles of blue-green algae is that it has revolutionized the field of agriculture microbiology due to the use of cyanobacterial biofertilizers. The important genera are *Anabaena, Nostoc, Aulosira, Calothrix, Tolypothrix*, etc.

b. Actinomycetes: Actinomycetes are a large group of bacteria that share the characters of both bacteria and fungi, and they are commonly known as "ray-fungi" because they grow as hyphae like fungi. They are Gram-positive and release antibiotic substances. However, they are responsible for the "earthy" odor of newly wetted soil. It grows luxuriantly in the neutral or alkaline pH (6.0 to 8.0). Some of the important members of actinomycetes: *Actinomyces, Actinoplanes, Microbispora, Streptomyces, Thermoactinomyces*, etc.

c. Fungi: Fungi are organisms but neither plant nor animal. They are helpful but could also be harmful to soil organisms. Fungi are helpful because they have the ability to break down nutrients and release them into the soil that other organisms cannot. Fungi can attach themselves to plant roots which helps plants to grow better and this relationship is called mycorrhiza. Some decomposers (saprophytic fungi) are: *Alternaria, Aspergillus, Cladosporium, Helminthosporium, Metarrhizium*, etc. On the other hand, fungi can get food by being parasites, attaching themselves to plants or other organisms. They act like pathogens. Fungi that are associated with plant disease are: *Armillaria, Fusarium, Phytophthora, Rhizoctonia, Sclerotium, Verticillium*, etc.

d. Protozoa: In moist soil, most of the members of microfauna remain in encysted form. Protozoa are one cell and microscopic organisms that larger than bacteria. They are grouped by the ways they move: amoebae use a pseudo (fake) foot, ciliates have cilia (short hair), and flagellates have one or more flagella (whips) and move them

Introduction

very fast. Protozoa are important for mineralizing nutrients and making them available for plants and other soil organisms. Protozoa eat bacteria and get carbon from them as well releasing excess nitrogen in the form of ammonium (NH^{4+}) near the root system of a plant, and thereby regulate bacterial populations. However, the number of protozoa can be correlated with plant root growth and indirectly with the status of soil nutrients. Examples are: *Colpoda, Pleurotricha, Heteromita, Cercomonas, Oikomonas*, etc.

1.7.   Future Prospects

Today, microbial diversity is a significant member of the worldwide business and its role is valuable (Sanchez, 2005). This will remain a big challenge for new technology to assign functions for microorganisms. It has been known for very nearly one hundred years that microorganisms could produce powerful utility, but only in the past few years has this capability become more than a laboratory novelty (Heilmann and Logan, 2006). The future microbial commitment is probably going to get more prominent in medical issues, for example, for example, cancers (Feling *et al.*, 2003), neurological (Rothstein *et al.*, 2005), and resistant ailments (Pham *et al.*, 2007). The diversity of microorganisms is very essential and potential; an important element in the development of new drugs for health care and disease control in the Pharmaceutical industries. Microbes are essential for numerous essential functions for the biosphere that include nutrient cycling (Hu *et al.*, 2006) and environmental detoxification (Carepo *et al.*, 2004). The immense range of microbial processes with their importance to the biosphere and the human economies provide a strong rationale for understanding their diversity, conservation, and exploitation for society. It should be emphasized that a molecular ecology is a valuable tool. Advances in molecular strategies have given us a brief look at the gigantic variety present inside the microbial world, however noteworthy work remains to be done to understand the ecological and evolutionary dynamics that can account for the origin, preservation, and distribution of that diversity (Cohan and Perry, 2007).

1.8. Objectives of the Study

Efforts have been made to analyze soil from Mehsana and Narmada District undertaking the following objectives:

1. To analyze and evaluate nutrient contents of agriculture soil of Mehsana and Narmada Districts.
2. Isolation, Screening, and characterization (sequencing) of soil microbial mass from the selected regions.
3. To rejuvenate agriculture soil by incorporation of selected microorganisms for enhancement of fertility and productivity.

Chapter 2

Review of Literature

2.0 Review of Literature

In today's agriculture, there has been a growing conviction that organic soil amendment is the best available option for restoration and enhancement of potential soil to restrict the continuous decline of productivity (Bhattacharya and Chakraborty, 2005; Hornick and Parr, 1987). Research has conclusively established that long-term application of organic manure competes well in production with direct application of chemical fertilizer (Briggs and Courtney, 1985). Simultaneously, manure application has likewise been found to impact the microbial-induced suppression of soil-borne plant pathogens and diseases (Hadar and Mandelbaum, 1992; Hoitink *et al.*, 1991). Apart from that, compost plays an important role in the breakdown of pesticides in soil. According to Fogarty and Tuovinen, 1991, some microorganisms, which rely on the feedstock for food and energy, may co-metabolize pesticides, while breaking down an adjacent pesticide.

2.1. Soil Quality

The soil quality concept change as we become aware of the many essential functions which soil performs in the biosphere, in addition to serving as a medium for plant growth, and as societal priorities change. In the late seventies of the twentieth century, Warkentin and Fletcher, 1977 discussed the evolution of soil quality concepts in intensive agriculture. The oldest and most frequently used concept was one of 'suitability for chosen uses', with emphasis on capability to support crop growth or engineering structures. Another stage in this evolution was the development of the intrinsic value' concept of soil. Historically, the soil has been utilized as a waste disposal system. However, in the 1960s and 1970s, it became increasingly apparent that soils were receiving wastes of a type, and at a rate, that overwhelmed their assimilative capacity. This trend threatened soil function and called for work in defining soil quality criteria (Doran *et al.*, 1994; Doran and Jones, 1996). Soil quality is largely defined by the ability of soil to perform various intrinsic and extrinsic functions. Blum and Santelises, 1994 have described a concept of sustainability and soil resilience based on six main soil functions; three are ecological and the other three are related to human activity. Ecological functions include: (a) biomass production, (b) soil as a reactor that filters, buffers, and transforms matter, and (c) biological habitat and genetic reserve. Functions linked to human activity include: (a) physical medium, serving as a spatial base for technical and industrial structures and socio-economic activities (b) source of raw materials, and (c) part of our cultural heritage that preserves the history of earth and humankind.

Similarly, soil quality is represented by a set-up of physical, chemical, and biological properties together (Doran *et al.*, 1994). Soil serves as a medium for plant growth by providing physical support, water, essential nutrients, and oxygen for roots. The capacity of soil to store and transmit water is a central point, controlling water accessibility to plants and transport of environmental pollutants to surface and groundwater (Paul and Clark, 1996). Much like air and water, soil quality profoundly affects the health and productivity of any given biome, and the associated environment and ecosystems. In other words, as a natural body, the soil has significance and incentive in itself not really as characterized by its managed applications. These contemplations led to the following definition: "Soil quality is the capacity of soil to function, within the ecosystem and land-use limits, to sustain biological productivity, maintain environmental quality and promote plant, animal and human health" (Doran *et al.*, 1994; Hatfield and Stewart, 1994; Lal, 1998).

2.2. Soil Health

Soil health is defined as the, "continued capacity of soil to function as a vital living system, within the ecosystem and land-use boundaries, to sustain biological productivity, maintain environmental quality and promote plant, animal, and human health (Doran and Safley, 1997; Bezdicek, 1996). Soil health can be viewed as a subset of ecosystem health. The concept of soil health and soil quality has reliably advanced with an expansion in the comprehension of soil and its quality characteristics. There is a need to contemplate soil health. Soil quality cannot be measured directly, but soil properties can be used as indicators. Biomarkers/bio-indicators are very sensitive to the environmental changes encompassing not only soil physical and chemical factors but also microbial, biochemical, and molecular attributes.

a. Soil health indicators: According to USDA soil quality indicators are classified into four categories that include: (a) visual indicators can be obtained through field visits, perception of farmers, and local knowledge. For example, observation or photographic interpretation, subsoil exposure, erosion, presence of weeds, color, type of coverage, etc. (b) physical indicators are related to the organization of the particles and pores; they include depth, bulk density, porosity, texture, etc. (c) chemical indicators include pH, salinity, organic matter content, phosphorus availability, nutrient cycling, and the presence of contaminants such as heavy metals, organic compounds, radioactive substances, etc. (d) biological indicators include estimations of microorganisms and macro-organisms, their activities or functions (Anderson, 2003). Biological indicators additionally incorporate metabolic processes such as respiration, chemical compounds, or metabolic products of organisms (Dick, 2000). Several soil bioindicators for soil health and its quality have been developed and reviewed (Nielsen and Winding, 2002; Anderson, 2003; Doran and Ziess, 2000; Cantu *et al.*, 2007).

b. Soil organic matter: Soil organic matter (SOM) is primarily plant residues, in different stages of decomposition. Soil organic carbon (SOC) is the most important indicator of soil quality (Magdoff and van Es, 2000; Kowaljow and Mazzarino, 2007). It is directly related to the maintenance of soil structure, presence of different groups of micro-organisms, mineralization of organic matter, and nutrient availability. However, SOM content varies with changes in climate, soil, and crop management (Nichols, 1984).

c. Soil respiration: Soil respiration parameter is strongly affected by the physiological state of microorganisms and nutrient availability. It depends on the physical and chemical properties like temperature, soil moisture, density, and pH. Nonetheless, respiration is considered a sensitive soil microbial parameter. The soil respiration without the addition of any substrate or nutrients i.e. basal respiration (BR) is the elementary parameter of usual soil microbial assessment and monitoring (Eisentraeger *et al.*, 2000).

d. Enzyme activity: Soil enzymes are important in the overall process of organic matter decomposition by catalyzing several reactions, necessary for the life processes of micro-organisms in soil (Ebersberger *et al.*, 2003; Kandeler *et al.*, 2006). Thus, they have been studied as indicators of soil quality (Gelsomino, 2006). Soil enzymes like amylase, β-glucosidase, cellulose, chitinase, dehydrogenase, phosphatase, protease, and urease have a very potent role in the ecosystem. Authors such as Dick *et al.,* 1996, Nielsen and Winding (2002); and Eldor (2007), report enzymes as good indicators because: (a) they are closely related to organic matter, physical characteristics, microbial activity, and biomass in the soil, (b) provide early information about changes in quality, and are more rapidly assessed.

2.3. Soil and Biodiversity

Biodiversity is described as a function of two components: (a) the total number of species present, i.e. species richness or species abundance, and (b) the distribution of individuals among those species i.e. species evenness or species equitability. However, our knowledge about the biodiversity of the soil biota which contributes to soil functional processes remains poor because of technical difficulties associated with sampling and quantifying the biodiversity of soil organisms (Pankhurst *et al.,* 1996). Biodiversity is an expression of genetic, species, and ecosystem-level variety of living things. From the molecular point of view, diversity often refers to the number of different sequence types present in a habitat, e.g., soil (Borneman *et al.,* 1996; Dunbar *et al.,* 1999; 2000). And diversity changes can give valuable information about the Physico-chemical properties of the soil. Therefore, soil biodiversity, including microbial diversity, could be used as an indicator of soil quality (Pankhurst *et al.,* 1997).

2.4. Soil Physico-Chemical Analysis

The proper plant growth requires a total of 17 essential elements. The essential nutrients are listed in Table-2.1, can result in severe damage to crop health. Of the mineral elements, the primary macronutrients (nitrogen, phosphorous, and potassium) are needed in the greatest quantities and are most likely to be in short supply in agricultural soils. Secondary macronutrients are needed in smaller quantities and are typically found in sufficient quantities in agricultural soil, and therefore do not often limit crop growth. Micronutrients, or trace nutrients, are needed in very small amounts and can be toxic to plants in excess. Silicon (Si) and sodium (Na) are sometimes considered essential plant nutrients, but due to their ubiquitous presence in soils, they are never in short supply (Parikh and James, 2012). Agriculture alters the natural cycling of nutrients in the soil. Intensive cultivation and harvesting of crops for human or animal consumption can effectively deplete the soil of plant nutrients. So, it is important to analyze soil. Soil analysis gives the idea to understand the

Review of Literature

fertility as well as the health of the soil. Physical and Chemical parameters of soil are described below which are important to understand for better agricultural soil quality and health.

Essential Plant Element		Symbol	Primary Form
Non-Mineral Elements	Carbon	C	$CO_2(g)$
	Hydrogen	H	$H_2O(l)$, H^+
	Oxygen	O	$H_2O(l)$, $O_2(g)$
Mineral Elements			
Primary Macronutrients	Nitrogen	N	NH_4^+, NO_3^-
	Phosphorus	P	HPO_4^{2-}, $H_2PO_4^-$
	Potassium	K	K^+
Secondary Macronutrients	Calcium	Ca	Ca^{2+}
	Magnesium	Mg	Mg^{2+}
	Sulfur	S	SO_4^{2-}
Micronutrients	Iron	Fe	Fe^{3+}, Fe^{2+}
	Manganese	Mn	Mn^{2+}
	Zinc	Zn	Zn^{2+}
	Copper	Cu	Cu^{2+}
	Boron	B	$B(OH)_3$
	Molybdenum	Mo	MoO_4^{2-}
	Chlorine	Cl	Cl^-
	Nickel	Ni	Ni^{2+}

(*Source*: Parikh and James, 2012)

Table-2.1: Essential Plant Nutrient Elements and their primary form utilized by Plants

2.4.1. Moisture: A small proportion (only 0.15%) of the liquid freshwater is available on Earth as soil moisture (Dingman, 1994), and that is influential water storage in the hydrologic cycle. It modulates interactions between the land surface and the atmosphere, thereby influencing climate and weather (Entekhabi, 1995; Dunne *et al.*, 1975). Soil moisture influences a variety of processes related to plant growth (and hence ecological patterns (Rodriguez - Iturbe, 2000) and agricultural production), as well as a range of soil processes (Brady, 1990; White, 1997).

2.4.2. Bulk Density (BD): Various studies have shown the soil compaction effects on the establishment and growth of plants (Lull, 1959; Foil and Ralston, 1967; Hatchell *et al.*, 1970; Wilshire *et al.*, 1978; Froehlich, 1979; Greacen and Sands, 1980; Wert and Thomas, 1981). This complex interaction between appears due to the higher soil bulk density that inhibits the root penetration and growth (O'Connell, 1975). Growth-limiting bulk density (GLBD) is influenced by many soil properties

Review of Literature

especially soil texture (Veihmeyer and Hendrickson, 1948; Schuurman, 1965; O'Connell, 1975). The main reason why soil texture strongly influences GLBD is its effect on soil pore size and mechanical resistance.

2.4.3. Texture: The physical arrangement of the soil solids dictates the distribution possibilities of the liquid and gaseous components within soil pores or pore space. This pore size may be determined by the arrangement of the primary soil particles that also reveal soil structure. Soil structure determines the size, shape, and arrangement of the pore space between and within aggregates. The relative proportions of sand, silt, and clay-sized materials present in a soil determine its textural characteristics. For a particular soil, maintenance of and improvements to the existing structure will come through optimizing the organic matter content and the species diversity activity of the soil biota (Lal, 1994).

2.4.4. pH: Soil pH is the measure of the H^+ ion activity of the soil-water system. It indicates the acidic, neutral, or alkaline nature of the soil. A soil pH ($CaCl_2$) of 5.2 to 8.0 provides optimum conditions for most agricultural plants. All plants are affected by the extremes of pH but there is wide variation in their tolerance of acidity and alkalinity. Some plants grow well over a wide pH range, whilst others are very sensitive to small variations in acidity or alkalinity.

2.4.5. Electrical Conductivity (EC): Electrical conductivity is the ability of a material to transmit (conduct) an electrical current. Rhoades *et al.*, 1989 presented a soil electrical conductivity model and assumed the specific EC of a soil containing dissolved electrolytes (salts). The measurement of EC can be directly related to the soluble salts concentration of the soil at any particular temperature. Furthermore, the existence of some ions in the moisture-filled soil pores changes soil EC value in the same way that salinity does; and that show the relationship between soil electrical conductivity and salinity level such as in (Eigenberg and Nienaber, 1998; 1999; 2001; Mankin and Karthikeyan, 2002; Herrero *et al.*, 2003; Paine, 2003; Kaffka *et al.*, 2005; Doerge *et al.*, 1999; Mcbride *et al.*, 1990 and Triantafilis *et al.*, 2002).

2.4.6. Organic Carbon/Matter (OC): Organic matter in soils and sediments is widely distributed over the earth's surface (Schnitzer, 1978). Naturally occurring organic carbon forms derive from the decomposition of biological debris. In the study of carbon and soil organic matter, a positive correlation was found (Schuur *et al.*, 2001; Leng *et al.*, 2009). This suggests that the soil organic matter is a source of carbon that is stored in the soil profiles (Brady and Weil, 2002). Total carbon is high at 0 to 20 cm indicates a higher decomposition of biomass. Numerous comparison studies have been performed examining the efficiency of total organic carbon methods i.e. Tinsley method, Bremner & Jenkinson 1960, Walkley-Black method (Nelson and Sommers, 1996).

2.4.7. Nitrogen (N): All forms of life on earth require energy, nutrition, and water for their growth like nitrogen (N). N is a basic constituent (proteins, nucleic acids) of all vital biological processes as well as also a basic constituent of many other compounds of primary physiological importance to plant metabolism, such as chlorophyll, nucleotides, proteins, alkaloids, enzymes, hormones, and vitamins (Marschner, 1995). Microorganisms play a key role in determining the nitrogen available for plant growth and crop production (Stevenson, 1982; Jenkinson and Smith, 1988; Wilson, 1988; Powlson *et al.*, 1998). Mineral nitrogen N is highly mobile and it can be lost through leaching (Jenkinson, 1990; Hauck, 1990; Diaz and Rosenberg, 2008). So, for balanced and proper agricultural systems management of external sources of nitrogen is important (Vanlauwe *et al.*, 2002). About 95 % of nitrogen is found in undisturbed natural soil organic matter (Walworth, 2013). Natural sources of nitrogen include those found sequestered in soils via mineralization and bacterial fixation (Hurek *et al.*, 1995; Ma *et al.*, 2015; Vinod *et al.*, 2016, Hocking and Reynolds, 2012; Nogalska, 2013; Sharma *et al.*, 2017). Two methods have gained acceptance for the determination of total nitrogen one is The Kjeldahl method (1883) and the Dumas method (1831).

2.4.8. Phosphorus (P): Phosphorus is an essential element for all living organisms. As a component of every living cell, P cannot be replaced by any other element in many physiological and biochemical processes. It is a second key nutrient found in the soil and ranking 11th in order of abundance in the earth's crust. The amount of P available to plants is generally not exceeding 0.01 % of the total P. The total-P in the soil is found between 0.02 to 0.10 % by weight and that is in two forms: Organic-P (20 to 28 %) and the rest is inorganic P (Devlin and Witham, 1983). In soil testing work, the available phosphorus content can be readily determined by Bray's No.1

method (pH around 5.5 or less) for acidic soil, and 2) Olsen's method is for slightly acidic, neutral, and calcareous soil.

2.4.9. Potassium (K): Potassium is the seventh most abundant element in the earth's crust. Liebig, 1841 was the first to recognize that it is essential for plant growth. Potassium has been described as the "quality element" for crop production (Usherwood, 1985). K is involved in the neutralization of charges, and the most important inorganic osmotic active substances in plant cells and tissues (Clarkson and Hanson, 1980; Marschner, 1995). K exists as a free ion in solution or as an electrostatically bound cation. With a shortage of K many metabolic processes are affected, like the rate of photosynthesis and the rate of translocation and enzyme systems (Läuchli and Pflüger, 1978; Marschner, 1995; Mengel and Kirkby, 1987; Mengel, 1997) while at the same time, the rate of dark respiration is increased. The result is a reduction in plant growth and quality. And the presence of K is estimated by the Flame Photometric method.

2.4.10. Micronutrients: Zink (Zn), Copper (Cu), Iron (Fe) and Manganese (Mn): The most commonly studied micronutrients are Zn, Cu, Fe, and Mn. It is important to assess the present micronutrient status because micronutrient deficiency has a direct impact on crop production and human health. About 48 percent of Indian soils are deficient in zinc, 11.2 percent in iron, 7 percent in copper, and 5.1 percent in manganese (Gupta, 2005). Micronutrients are present in different forms in the soil. Zink as Zn^{2+} and Copper as Cu^{2+} are present as divalent cations in the soil, Iron is present insoluble ferric oxide and Manganese originates primarily from the decomposition of ferromagnesian rocks. It is taken up by the plants as Mn^{2+} ions, although it exists in many oxidation states. Different extractant methods have been developed for assessing plant available nutrient content in the soils. The elements can be estimated by Lindsay and Norvell, 1978 method.

2.5.   Soil as a Habitat for Microorganism and its role in Soil Quality

Microbes have played key roles in Earth's climatic, geological, geochemical, and biological evolution (Xu, 2006). The prokaryotic life emerged about 3.8 billion years ago; about 2 billion years before eukaryotic life arose and have provided conditions on the planet that have made it habitable for all other species

(Das *et al.*, 2006). Furthermore, microbial life is widely distributed: where there is life on earth, there is microbial life (Xu, 2006). Their activity is important in maintaining soil aggregate stability and good soil structure (Paul and Clark, 1996; Chenu and Stotzky, 2002). Soil pores are filled with water and gases and the concentration of individual gases within soil fabric is a function of both biotic and abiotic microbial processes (Paul and Clark, 1996). Soil temperature and redox potential are also important for microorganism activities that follow or as per the laws of thermodynamics (Sparks, 1995; Paul and Clark, 1996).

2.5.1. The usefulness of Soil Microorganisms (Why we need Soil Microbes?)

All-natural soils contain vast populations of organisms and all compete with each other for food and space. Among them, microorganisms are a very important link to survive on the earth for the rest of the organisms. Microbes break down a variety of carbon and energy sources into small molecules into primary metabolites (Sanchez, 2005) and some microbial species are also able to produce secondary metabolites which are not essential for growth; those are important mediators of ecological interactions between organisms and their environment (Lokvam *et al.*, 2006). The majority of bacteria and fungi present in soils are considered to be beneficial to higher plants by (1) direct association with plant roots, (2) breakdown and release of minerals, (3) parasitizing or disease-causing microorganisms or, (4) suppressing growth (Ranjan *et al.*, 2005; Sharma *et al.*, 2005; Ting *et al.*, 2004, Kalia *et al.*, 2003 a, b; Reddy *et al.*, 2003; Kalia and Purohit, 2008). New tools are accessing microbial diversity to provide novel genes and biosynthetic pathways that can be commercialized to replace the overuse of industrial-made chemical-like substances (Losada *et al.*, 2007; Jiang and Wu, 2007; Kalia *et al.*, 2007). Uses for microbes and microbial products appear to be nearly endless.

a. Nitrogen Fixing Bacteria (NFB): Air contains approximately 79 % nitrogen, but plants cannot use it. The conversion of N_2 into the absorbable compound by the microorganisms for the plants is known as nitrogen fixation and microorganisms are called Biofertilizers. Nitrogen-fixing organisms are Aerobic (require oxygen for growth and fix nitrogen), Free-living (fix nitrogen both in aerobic and anaerobic conditions), and Symbiotic (fix nitrogen only by the formation of nodules) (Wakayama *et al.*, 2000). The family Azotobacteriaceae comprises of two genera namely, *Azomonas* sp. (non-cyst forming) and *Azotobacter* sp. (cyst forming). *Azotobacter* sp. is generally regarded as a free-living aerobic nitrogen-fixer. *Azotobacter* sp. was originally used as seed inoculants because it was the nitrogen economy of plants (Cooper, 1959). The cells of *Azotobacter* sp. are Gram-negative, oval and spherical 2 - 10 µm × 1 -2 µm in size, motile aerobic soil-dwelling bacteria. The Azotobacter sp. produces substances like Indole acetic acid (IAA) and Gibberellic acid in the bioassay. They are grown in media such as Ashby's medium, Jensen's nitrogen-free medium, and Waksman's base medium.

b. Phosphate Solubilizing Bacteria (PSB): Phosphorus plays a key role in all life forms (Behera *et al.*, 2017). It is essential for several plant physiological activities like photosynthesis, cell division, and others (Guptaa *et al.*, 2012). Applied inorganic chemical fertilizer phosphate to the soil rapidly becomes unavailable to plants (Yadav and Dadarwal, 1997). To overcome this serious problem, natural phosphate solubilization by different microorganisms is, therefore, important (Vassileva *et al.*, 2010; Banerjee *et. al.*, 2010; Martınez *et al.*, 2010). Phosphate solubilizing bacteria (PSB) which is associated with plant roots is one of the most significant alternatives for inorganic phosphate fertilizers (Thakuria *et al.*, 2004; Mahmood *et al.*, 2010; Mamta *et al.*, 2011; Mamta *et al.*, 2010). Phosphate solubilizing bacteria are grown in Pikovskaya's agar medium.

c. Potassium Solubilizing Bacteria (KSB): Potassium is the seventh most common element in the earth s crust. In Indian soil, the soluble K is approximately 2% and insoluble is 98% in form of minerals like biotite, feldspar, mica, muscovite, vermiculite (Goldstein, 1994). Different bacterial species are solubilizing potassium (Muentz, 1890; Archana, 2013; Aleksandrov, 1967). Potassium solubilizing bacteria *Bacillus mucilaginosus* can solubilize rock Potassium mineral powder such as micas, illite, and orthoclases through the production and excretion of organic acids (Ullaman, 1996). They are grown in Aleksandrow Agar medium.

2.5.2. Soil Microbial Diversity

Biodiversity would be the total genetic information on Earth while diversity would be the active and abundant components at one particular time and place (Alio, 2006b). In general terms, microbial diversity includes genetic diversity, that is, the amount and distribution of genetic information, within microbial species; diversity of bacterial species in microbial communities (Nannipieri *et al.*, 2003). The microbial world is the largest unexplored reservoir of biodiversity on the earth and bacteria are the least understood in terms of their diversity, physiologies, and ecological panorama (Woese *et al.*, 1990, Rappe *et al.*, 2003). Current evidence suggests that there may be 300000 to 1 million species on earth yet only 3100 bacteria are described in Bergey's Manual, the treatise of described bacteria (Report of a workshop held at Michigan State University, sponsored by Bergey's Manual Trust, August 1995). Soil is a complex, dynamic, and living habitat for a large number of organisms. Bacteria are an important part of the soil microflora because of their abundance of up to 10^9 cells per gram of soil (Daniel, 2004, Torsvik *et al.*, 1990a), and play a key role in the biogeochemical cycles (Paul and Clark, 1996). Microorganisms are also present in surface seawater (Sogin *et al.*, 2006).

Habitat Culturability[a]	(%) Values
Seawater	0.001-0.1
Mesotrophic lake	0-1
Unpolluted estuarine waters	0.1-3
Freshwater	0.25
Sediments	0.25
Soil	0.3
Activated sludge	1-15
a: Culturable bacteria are measured as Colony Forming Unit (CFU).	
b: Culturable bacteria in comparison with total cell counts.	

(*Source*: Amann *et al.*, 1995)

Table-2.2: Bacterial Culturability among Various Habitats

More than 99 % of prokaryotes in the environment cannot be cultured in the laboratory (Schloss and Handelsman, 2005b). The term "the great plate count anomaly" was coined by Staley and Konopka (1985) to describe the difference between the cell numbers from natural environments that form colonies on agar media and the numbers countable by microscopic examination (Amann *et al.*, 1995). Culturability determined as a percentage of culturable bacteria in comparison with total cell counts observed among various habitats are shown in Table-2.2. Recent advances in the field of molecular biology (extraction of nucleic acids, polymerase chain reaction (PCR) amplification, DNA cloning, DNA sequencing) have made it much easier to study microbial diversity (Ranjard *et al.*, 2000).

2.5.3. Approaches to measuring the Soil Microbial Flora/Community

Studies of soil microbial properties have been commonly conducted at the process level but less attention are given to the community-level or organism-level responses to changes in soil properties (Weaver et al., 1994; Hill et al., 2000; 2003). These process-level measurements are limited in their ability to describe a particular microbial ecosystem while community-level microbial interactions are more complex (Pankhurst et al., 1997). Many new methods and approaches are now available to study microbial flora that could be divided into two categories: (a) Culture-dependent Methods and (b) Culture-independent Methods (van Elsas, et al., 1997; Ranjard et al., 2000; Hill et al., 2000; Giraffa and Neviani, 2001).

2.5.3.1. Culture-Dependent Methods of Community Analysis

a. Dilution Plating and Culturing Methods: Traditional analysis method that depends on culturing techniques and media designed (Weaver et al., 1994). These techniques have revealed a diversity of microorganisms associated with various soil conditions, such as disease suppression and organic matter decomposition (Tunlid et al., 1989; Boehm et al., 1993; 1997; de Leij et al., 1993; de Brito Alvarez et al., 1995; Hu & van Bruggen, 1997; Maloney et al., 1997).

b. Community-Level Physiological Profiles: One of the more widely used culture-dependent methods for community-level physiological profiles of soil microorganisms (Garland & Mills, 1991; Zak et al., 1994; Konopka et al., 1998). In this traditional bacterial taxonomy method, community-level physiological profiles have been facilitated by the use of a commercial taxonomic system, known as the BIOLOG® system (Hill et al., 2000). This system is based on the utilization of 95 different carbon sources and can be useful in assessing gross functional diversity (Garland and Mills, 1991; Haack et al., 1995; Garland, 1997; Smalla et al., 1998; Zak et al., 1994; Garland, 1996a; b; Campbell et al., 1997).

2.5.3.2. Culture-Independent Methods of Community Analysis

Soil microbial ecologists are turning increasingly on culture-independent methods of community analysis because of the inherent limitations of culture-based methods. Culture-independent studies include phospholipid fatty acids and nucleic acids analysis (Morgan and Winstanley, 1997).

a. Phospholipid Fatty Acid (PLFA) Analysis: In the method, assessing the structure of soil microbial communities and determining gross changes that accompany soil disturbances such as cropping practices (Zelles *et al.*, 1992; Zelles, 1999), pollution (Frostegard *et al.*, 1993), fumigation (Macalady *et al.*, 1998), and changes in soil quality (Bardgett *et al.*, 1996; Reichardt *et al.*, 1997; Bossio *et al.*, 1998; Petersen *et al.*, 1998). PLFA is a signature molecule and found exclusively in cell membranes and not in other parts of the cell that is the important indicator of active microbial biomass (Tunlid and White, 1992; Zelles and Bai, 1993).

b. DNA-Based Techniques: Here, nucleic acids providing a new understanding of the structure of microbial communities. By isolating the sequence diversity of the DNA, researchers estimated that the genetic diversity of soil was 200 times greater than the diversity among bacteria cultured from the same soil. DNA sequences may provide a greater understanding of the microbial diversity that exists in soil than could be gained from culture-dependent methods (Torsvik *et al.*, 1990a; b; Ovreas and Torsvik, 1998; Torsvik *et al.*, 1998).

Numerous studies have applied these techniques to soil microbial communities study (e.g. Lee et al., 1996; Stephen et al., 1996; Ueda et al., 1995; Borneman et al. 1996; Rheims et al., 1996; Bintrim et al., 1997; Borneman and Triplett, 1997; Felske et al., 1996, Felske and Akkermans, 1998a; b; Heuer and Smalla, 1997; Kuske et al., 1997; Smith et al., 1997; Duineveld et al., 1998; Grosskopf et al., 1998; Dunbar et al., 1999; Rondon et al., 2000) and novel microbial lineages have been discovered. For example, studies have shown that agricultural soils contain a diversity of Archaea, organisms previously thought to exist only in extreme environments (Ueda et al., 1995; Bintrim et al., 1997; Buckley et al., 1998).

2.6. Molecular study

The DNA sequence of the 16S rDNA gene has been determined for an extremely large number of species. Carl Woese proposed the three domains system of classification - Archaea, Bacteria, and Eucarya - based on such sequence information (Fig.-2.1). Subsequently, several authors have identified/constructed, and published phylogenetic trees based on 16S rRNA gene sequences (Sass and Cypionka, 2004). Since the 1980s, the arrival of molecular techniques has provided many genotypic approaches to examine the taxonomy studies, including rRNA sequence comparison,

Review of Literature

DNA-DNA hybridization, and DNA fingerprinting (Song *et al.*, 2004). The function of the 16S rRNA gene over time has not changed, signifying that random sequence changes are a more precise measure of development. The length of the gene (1500 base pairs) is essential enough to release the information by bioinformatics tools. Therefore rRNA (rDNA) is extensively used for determining the taxonomy and phylogeny of recently isolated microorganisms. The rRNA genes are organized as a part of the multigene family and the copy number ranges from 1 to 15. The 16S rRNA sequence has hypervariable regions, where sequences have diverged over evolutionary time. Three regions within the 16S rRNA gene have been observed to have enough sequence variation to be useful for genus-specific (α & β regions) and species-specific (γ region) probes (Anderson *et al.*, 2001). These are often flanked by strongly-conserved regions. Primers are designed to bind to conserved regions and amplify variable regions. The 16S rRNA has properties, which predestine it as a universal phylogenetic marker. There are regions on the 16S rRNA that are quite conserved and others, which are variable. Hence genotypic classification based on nucleotide sequence comparison of 16S rRNA genes has become available as an additional taxonomic tool.

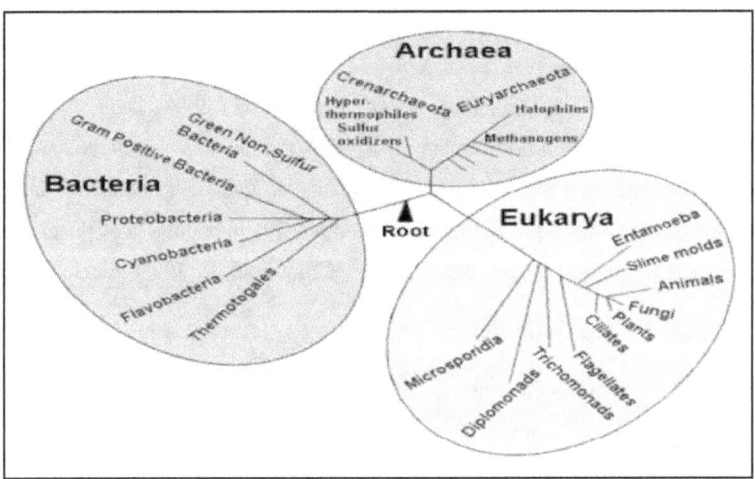

Fig.-2.1: Three Domain of Life

2.7. Soil Rejuvenation and Revitalization

Natural soil is thriving with life. They contain an incredible diversity of microscopic bacteria, fungi, viruses, and other organisms. To get more yields farmers rely increasingly on chemicals to replace biological soil functions but without a healthy microbial community, most of the nutrients are no longer recycled. Natural revitalization and artificial revitalization of soil are discussed below.

2.7.1. Naturally Revitalization (Humic Substances)

Soil rejuvenates naturally, the decaying of biological waste parts results in humus or humic acid. The chemical nature of humus is complex and the mechanism of its formation process is called "humification" (Senn and Alta, 1973). Humic substances are considered to play a crucial role in the terrestrial and aquatic systems that compose up to 80% of the soil organic matter (Tan, 2014; Brady and Weil, 2008). Humic substances, increase soil aggregation, water retention, infiltration rate, and water-holding capacity of the soil (Brady and Weil, 2008; Stevenson, 1982; Swift, 1996; Weber *et al.*, 2018; Quilty, 2011). Soil aggregation promotes high infiltration rates, which reduce runoff and erosion (Sylvia, 1998). Humic substances enhance soil fertility by impacting the composition of microbial populations (Calvo, 2014).

2.7.2. Chemical Fertilizers vs. Biofertilizers

Today, Chemical fertilizers contain chemical substances and Biofertilizers contain living microorganisms that colonize in the rhizosphere both are available important to increase soil nutrients for a plant or crop growth (Muraleedharan *et al.*, 2010). Both the fertilizers have positive and negative effects. In the positive effect, chemical fertilizers are soluble and immediately available to plants, the lower price which makes it more popular with farmers. Biofertilizers are well-balanced nutrient supplying and enhance soil biological activity which helps keep plants healthy as well as encourage the growth of beneficial microorganisms and earthworms. On the negative side of the chemical fertilizers, overuse can result in leaching, pollution of water resources, destruction of microorganisms and beneficial insects, crop susceptibility to disease attack, acidification or alkalization of the soil, or reduction in soil fertility, all of which cause irreparable damage to the overall ecosystem. On the other side, biofertilizers are comparatively low in nutrient content, so a large volume is required for crop growth. They release nutrients slowly to meet crop requirements in a short time, hence some nutrient deficiency may occur and the cost is high compared to chemical fertilizers as well as short shelf life (Chen, 2006).

2.7.3. Soil Amendments Benefits

The use of soil amendments has the potential to protect human health and the environment. This approach offers the benefit of recycling to reclaim damaged or disturbed land rather than disposing of what is generally considered to be waste in landfills or by incineration.

a. Benefits of the revitalized land: It provides wildlife habitat, improved water quality in receiving streams, sequestering of carbon, reuses of devoid and damaged lands, and improves property values.

b. Benefits of amendments: It restores the soil health and structure, ecological function of soils as well as decreases bioavailability, leachability, and mobility of toxic pollutants and contaminants.

This research is to evaluate the agricultural soil quality of the dry northern and moist southern agro-climatic zone of the Gujarat state as well as the biological rejuvenation studies of it. Groups of microbes (more specific bacteria) were amended in the selected agricultural site of both the district where it is particularly efficient for revitalizing soil and recycling nutrients. Hence, healthier soil will make it possible to grow more food with fewer inputs that will be more profitable for farming as well as will protect our air and water.

Chapter 3
Materials and Methods

Materials and Methods

3.0 Materials and Methods

3.1. Geographical and Climatic Summary of Study Areas

The state of Gujarat lies on the western coast of India. Geographically Gujarat is located between 20°6' to 24°42' North latitude and 68°10' to 74°28' East longitude. Gujarat has spread across an area of 196077 sq. km. It covers 5.96% of the area of India (Gujarat Forest Statistics, 2011-12) with a coastline stretching over 1290 km along the Arabian Sea; Gujarat has the longest coastline among all Indian states. Gujarat has a very diverse climatic condition, dry northern region and moist in the southern part. Hence, Gujarat has different forest types (Annexure-1.1). As the Tropic of Cancer passes through the northern border of the state Gujarat, the state has an intensely hot or cold climate. But the Arabian Sea and the Gulf of Cambay in the west and the eastern forest-covered hills soften the rigors of climatic extremes. There are a total of 33 districts in the state, in which Mehsana (Fig.-3.1) and Narmada (Fig.-3.2) districts were studied. Here, district-wise geography, climatic condition, and LULC have described below. Land Use is commonly defined as a series of operations on land, carried out by humans, intending to obtain products and/or benefits through using land resources. Land Cover is commonly defined as the vegetation (natural or planted) or man-made constructions (buildings, etc.) that occur on the earth's surface. Water, ice, bare rock, sand, and similar surfaces also count as land cover.

3.1.1. Mehsana District

This research was conducted on the Mehsana district which is situated in the North part of the Gujarat state. The district is encompassed by 23.04 and 24.09 North Latitude and 71.87 and 75.97 East Longitude (Bhuvan, ISRO). It shares its border with five other districts of the state. While Banaskantha fringes it towards the north, Ahmedabad and Gandhinagar are situated towards its south. Patan and Surendranagar district borders Mehsana from the west with Sabarkantha lying in the eastern direction. The district altitude is 93 m. The district is divided into 10 talukas and further divided into 614 villages. Unjha is the famous agricultural trade center for fennel, isabgol, and cumin seeds. The district is the largest producer of lemon and fennel seeds while the third-largest producer of tomatoes in the state. Mostly flat sandy loam and medium black types of soil are found in the district. The slope in this region ranges from 0 to 1

Materials and Methods

%. The soil in this district is neutral in pH i.e. 6.5 to 7.5, low phosphorus content, and a medium level of organic carbon. But high potash content makes it quite better for agriculture. Some areas in Mehsana have alluvial soil with kankar pan soil and mild black cotton soil as well. The district, about 3343 sq. km, dry climate as it is situated in the northern part of the state, with a mean maximum temperature of 40.5°C and minimum of 9.04°C and average annual rainfall was 719 mm during the year 2013 - 2017 (Gujarat Forest Statistics, 2017-18). The important minerals in the district are Bentonite, Calcite, China clay, Limestone, Fire clay, and Granite, etc. (State Industrial Profile of Gujarat, 2012-13). Hathmati, Sabarmati, Khari, Meshwo, Vatrak, Mazum and Harnav are the main rivers. The major crops of Mehsana are Wheat, Bajara, Jowar, Cotton, Tobacco, Castor, Mustard, Sesamum, Cumin, Isabgol, Fennel, Groundnut, Brinjal, Potato, Tomatoes, Okra, Mango, Citrus, Sapota.

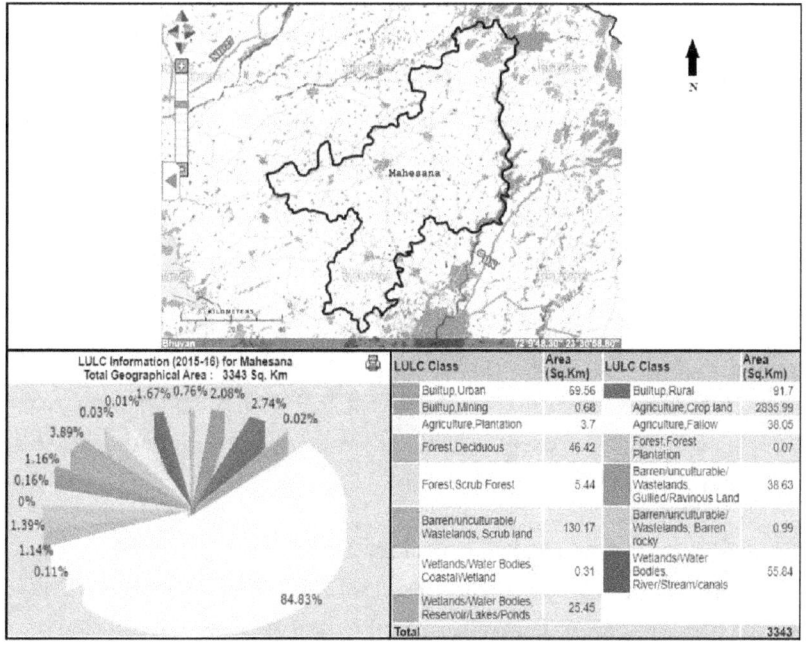

(*Source* - Bhuvan: ISRO/NRSC, 2019)
Fig.-3.1: Mehsana District Land Use Land Cover

3.1.1.1. Land Use Land Cover of the District

LULC for the Mehsana district, as per the Bhuvan: ISRO/NRSC, 2019

Materials and Methods

information which has appeared in (Fig.-3.1). The total geographical area of the district is 3343 sq. km. Agricultural cropland, fellow, and plantation cover 86.08 percent of the total district land. In a total of 161.94 sq. km. of buildup land, the urban area is 69.56 sq. km, the rural area is 91.7 sq. km and mining land is 0.68 sq. km. Moreover, the Deciduous and Scrub Forest covers 51.86 sq. km., and Forest Plantation is in 0.07 sq. km. Here, the barren and unbearable land distribution is 5.08 percent. And more than 2.40 percent of the district land is covered by the wetlands/water-body with incorporates rivers, streams, canals, reservoirs, lakes, and ponds.

3.1.2. Narmada District

This research was conducted on the Narmada district which is situated in the Southern part of the Gujarat state in India. The district is an administrative district in the southern part of the state. Geographically, it is located at 21.24 to 22 degrees North Latitude and 72.4 to 73.15 degrees East Longitude. This district was carved out on October 2, 1997. Nandod, Dediyapada and Sagbara talukas of Bharuch district and Tilakwada taluka of Vadodara district formed Narmada District. New taluka Garudeshwar was formed on 18/02/2014. The District is situated in the eastern corner of the Gujarat state. The district altitude is 417 m. It is spread across an area of 2794 sq km. The district is divided into 5 talukas and further divided into 562 villages. The climate of the Narmada district is dry and moist. The average temperature remains from 15 to 42°C. The average Rainfall here is 1100 mm. (Gujarat Forest Statistics, 2011-12). The main rivers of this district are Narmada, Karjan, Main, Ashwini, and Tarap. The major crops of Narmada are Cotton, Banana, Sugarcane, Pigeon Pea, Paddy, Pulses, Maize, and Sorghum.

3.1.2.1. Land Use Land Cover of the District

LULC for the Narmada district, as per the Bhuvan: ISRO/NRSC, 2019 information which has appeared in (Fig.-3.2). The total geographical area of the district is 2794 sq. km. Agricultural cropland, fellow, and plantation cover more than 50 percent of land use. In a total of 1.12 percent of buildup land, the urban area is 6.37 sq. km, the rural area is 24.55 sq. km and mining land is 0.21 sq. km. Moreover, the Deciduous and Scrub Forest covers 34.95 percent of land cover, and Forest Plantation

Materials and Methods

is in 2.96 sq. km. Here, the barren and unbearable land distribution 80.68 sq. km. And wetlands/water-bodies are in more than 8 percent, which incorporates rivers, streams, canals, reservoirs, lakes, and ponds.

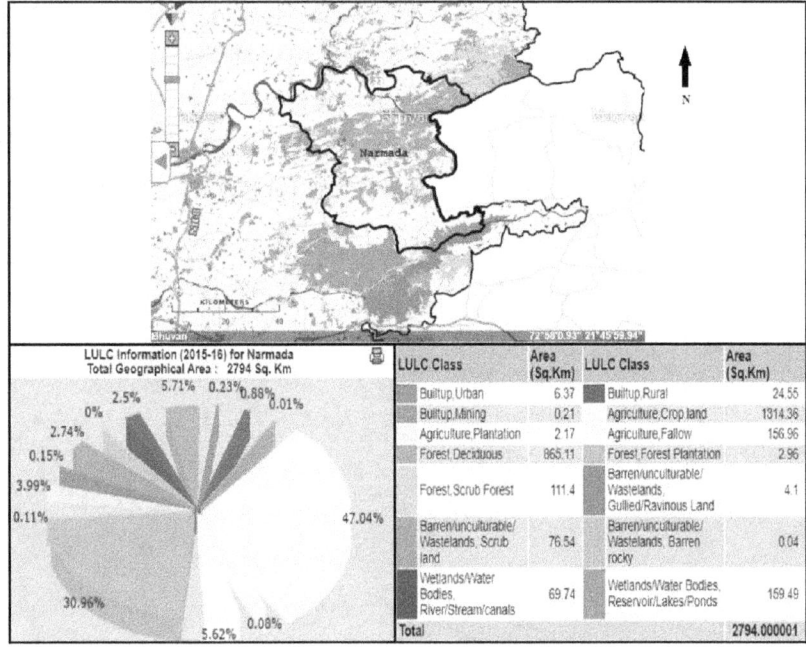

(*Source* - Bhuvan: ISRO/NRSC, 2019)
Fig.-3.2: Narmada District Land Use Land Cover

3.2. Soil Sampling

3.2.1. Random Soil Sampling with Q-GIS Lisboa

A geographic information system (GIS) is typically seen as a "toolbox" of commands for the input, analysis, storage, retrieval, and display of spatially related data (Tomlin, 1987). Bhuvan: ISRO/NRSC, 2019 information was utilized to make both the region's shapefile. After creating a district boundary shapefile, it was brought into the Quantum GIS 1.8.0 Lisboa a freeware. Firstly, Shapefiles of these two districts were included as a vector layer independently. In the software, Research Tools of the Vector menu was used to get or create Random Soil Sampling Points. The district boundary along with random points had shown in (Fig.-3.3) for Mehsana and (Fig.-3.5) for Narmada. Additionally, the information for topographical directions/

Materials and Methods

geographical coordinates of all random soil sampling points was recorded straightforwardly by copying Attribute Table into the MS-Word. Random soil sampling points were created as a layer on the District shapefile. So, there was another shapefile. All the shapefiles were changed over online into kmz. formate which is supported in Google Earth. Shapefiles of both the district were added into the Google Earth and were appeared in the beneath Images (Fig.-3.4 for Mehsana, Fig.-3.6 for Narmada). Landsat/ Copernicus data set of Google Earth was extremely useful to get the correct information about the sampling site. So, background analysis was useful for sampling.

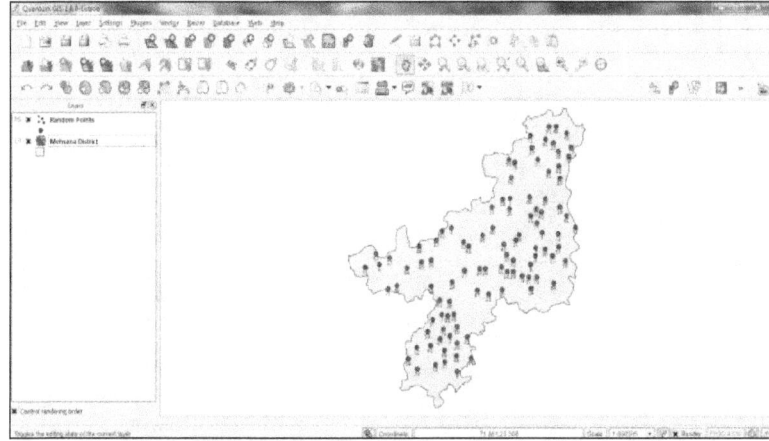

Fig.-3.3: Q-GIS based Random Soil Sampling for Mehsana District

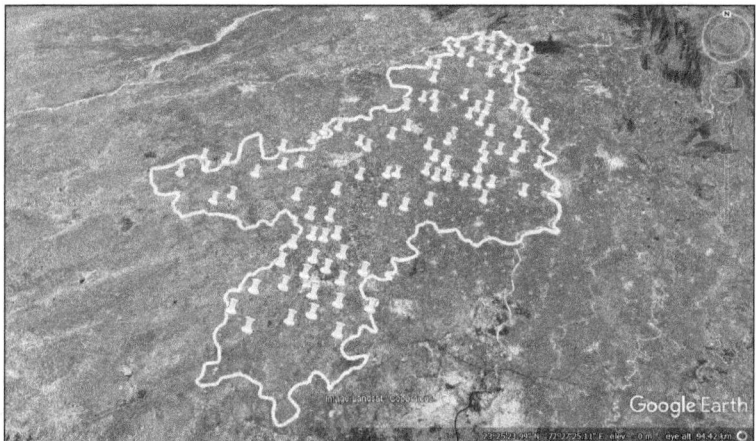

Fig.-3.4: Google Earth Image for Random Soil Sampling of Mehsana District

Materials and Methods

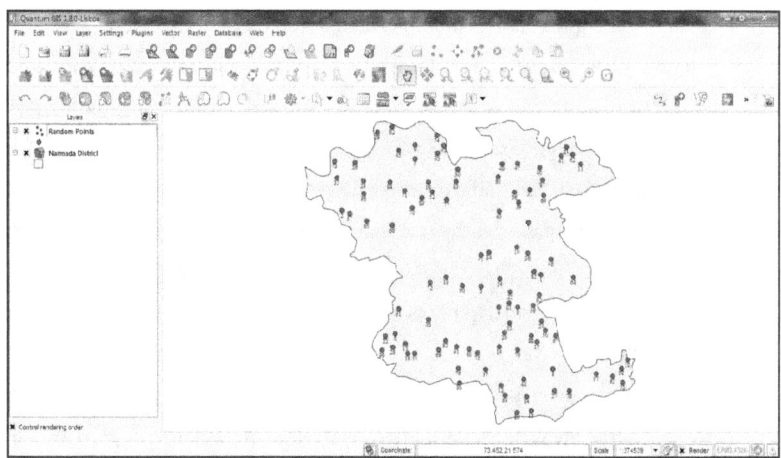

Fig.-3.5: Q-GIS based Random Soil Sampling for Narmada District

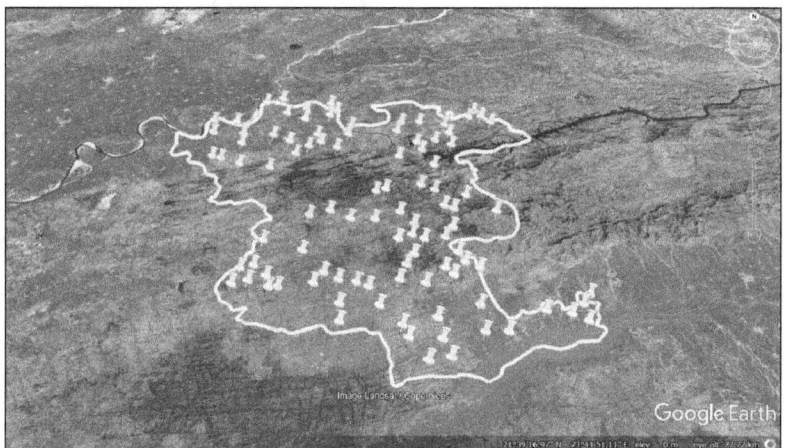

Fig.-3.6: Google Earth Image for Random Soil Sampling of Narmada District

3.2.2. Sample Collection

The soil sample was taken from the agricultural fields of both Mehsana and Narmada districts. The soil sample was taken in the fresh ziplock plastic bag and brought to the laboratory where the sample size was minimized and used for further work. The soil was air-dried at room temperature for physical and chemical analysis, while 10 gm of soil was kept at 4°C for microbiological work and that was not air-dried. After completion of the work, the excess amount of soil was discarded.

Materials and Methods

Sampling points were generated in the Q-GIS software. The software had given sample numbers 0 to 99 for a total of 100 samples. Based on the coordinates of the random points, the soil was collected. At some of the sites, the proper or exact location of the point sampling was impossible due to buildup land, city or village residential areas, water bodies, etc. As this study only focuses on the agricultural land, the soil was sampled nearby the random point location. The whole district was divided into 5 zones (North, South, East, West, and Middle). Zone wise soil sample was collected and further processed, analyzed, and stored. The soil study deals with the depth-wise variations in soil bacterial populations concerning the micro-environmental and soil nutrient variability in the Agricultural areas of both districts. Some studies dealt with depth effects (Arunachalam *et al.,* 1997) and others attempted to examine seasonal trends (Kennedy *et al.,* 2005). Therefore, Samples were taken at two depths and mixed. 0 to 15 cm depth was surface and 16 cm to 30 cm subsurface level. Before taking the sample, the upper surface was cleared by removing debris, dry leaf, etc., and collected in the plastic zip-lock bag (Fig.-3.7).

Fig.-3.7: Collection of Soil Sample

3.2.3. Samples at the Laboratory

After collecting the soil samples, it was promptly brought to the laboratory. The moisture content of the soil sample was analyzed, first. After that, they were dried at room temperature (Fig.-3.8). Then, dried samples were used for

Fig.-3.8: Air drying of Soil Sample

Materials and Methods

further laboratory explorations (soil physical and chemical analysis). Samples for Microbiological analysis were not air-dried. Those samples were kept at 4°C in the dark until analyses could be performed. Although this was an extended time for environmental samples to be stored, it is within the guidelines suggested by Anderson (1987) who recommended soil testing be performed within 3 months of collection. Tate, 1995 has indicated that the storage of soil at 4°C in the dark results in minimal changes in experimental data, even after several weeks.

3.3. Soil Physico-Chemical Assessment

3.3.1. Moisture Content (Gravimetric method)

This test was performed to determine the water (moisture) content of the Soil. The water content is the ratio, expressed as a percentage, of the mass of "pore" or "free" water in a given mass of soil to the mass of the dry soil solids. The method is based on removing soil moisture by oven-drying a soil sample until the weight remains constant. The moisture content (%) was calculated from the sample weight before and after drying.

Requirements: Moisture dish, drying oven, desiccator, analytical balance, gloves, and spatula

Procedure:

1. Moisture dish and lid number were recorded.
2. Mass of empty, clean, and dry moisture dish with its lid (W_1) was determined and recorded.
3. Moist soil was placed in the moisture dish and secured with the lid.

Fig.-3.9: Soil Moisture Content Dish

4. Mass of the moisture dish (now containing the moist soil) with the lid (W_2) was determined and recorded (Fig.-3.9).
5. The lid was removed and the moisture dish (containing the moist soil) was placed in the drying oven that was set at 105°C for overnight.
6. The moisture dish was removed from the oven. Carefully but securely, replaced

Materials and Methods

the lid on the moisture dish using gloves, and allowed it to cool to room temperature.

7. The mass of the moisture dish and lid (containing the dry soil) (W_3) was determined and recorded.

Calculation: Calculated the moisture content as a percentage of the dry soil weight,

$$\text{Soil Moisture (\%)} = \frac{(W_2 - W_3)}{(W_3 - W_1)} \times 100$$

Where: W_1 = weight of dish (g)

W_2 = weight of moist soil + dish (g)

W_3 = weight of dried soil + dish (g)

3.3.2. Measurement of Bulk Density

Soil bulk density is the ratio of the oven-dried mass of soil to its volume either at the time of sampling or at specified moisture content. It is usually expressed in terms of grams per cubic centimeter (g/cm^3) or SI units of megagram per cubic meter (Mg/m^3). Measurement of bulk density generally requires cores or clods in their natural structure. To obtain core samples is relatively simple if no stones are present; however, it is more difficult to obtain good quality cores. The core sampler is pushed or driven into the soil to the desired depth and then removed. If the soil sampler is assumed to be full its volume may be used as the volume of soil. If the sampler is not full an independent measurement must be made of the volume of soil. The bulk density or apparent gravity of soil is the mass of a unit volume of soil bulk including pore space.

Requirements: Oven, measuring cylinder or tube, and analytical balance

Procedure:

1. Few millimeters below the soil surface, the samples were dugout. Satisfactory scores

Fig.-3.10: Soil Bulk Density Testing

Materials and Methods

were packed in loose soil in plastic bags or other containers. Two or three cores might be placed in one plastic bag but, in this case, each core was wrapped in aluminum foil and transferred to the laboratory.

2. Soil core extruded into an aluminum tray and dried at a constant 105°C which might be required several days. Removal of the core might be assisted by partial drying as a preliminary treatment.
3. Then dry soil was transferred to a measuring cylinder/ tube that was already weighed and the internal volume of the tube was calculated in cubic centimeters from.
4. Recorded the weight of this volume of soil on a balance and calculated the Bulk Density (Fig.-3.10).

Calculation:

$$\text{Bulk Density } (g/cm^3) = \frac{\text{Weight of soil } (g)}{\text{Volume of soil } (cm^3)}$$

Precautions: Be careful while noting the value of weighing and drying soil.

3.3.3. Texture Analysis (U.S.D.A. method)

The pipette method is a standard method for particle size analysis and gives comparatively more accurate results. Soil fractions (1) Course sand > 0.2 mm diameter, (2) Fine sand 0.2 - 0.02 mm diameter, (3) Silt 0.02 - 0.002mm diameter and (4) Clay < 0.002 mm diameter can be determined by this method (Annexure-1.3).

Requirements: Balance and weight box, Cylinder (1 liter), Hot water-bath, Cover glass, 70 mm sieve, Dish and oven, Rubber pestle, Sedimentation cylinder, Shaker, Distilled water

Procedure:

1. A 70 mm mesh size sieve was placed on the mouth of the sedimentation cylinder.
2. The soil suspension was poured into the sieve, the material was washed with a stream of water to remove more clay and silt remained on the sieve and filled about half the cylinder.
3. Course material thus left on the sieve was transferred to a pre-weighed dish. Dried at 105°C and then weighted.

Materials and Methods

4. For separation of silt, the suspension was shaken well by repeated inversions of the cylinder. The sedimentation cylinder was kept still on the bench and the time of commencement of sedimentation was noted.
5. 25 ml suspension was withdrawn by a pipette fixed with a cork in such a manner that when cork rests on the top of the sedimentation cylinder, the tip of the pipette remains at the required distance below the surface of the suspension (10 cm in this case). That operation was started before 20 seconds - up i.e. 3 hours and 50 minutes.
6. The sample was taken into a pre-weighed dish, dried at 105°C, and weighed as silt+clay.
7. For separation of clay, the content was shaken for one minute by inversion of the cylinder.
8. 25 ml suspension was withdrawn in the same way at a depth of 10 cm after 6 hours and 20 minutes, dried at 105°C, ignited, and weighed.
9. For the separation of fine sand, the bulk of the supernatant liquid was poured away.
10. Now Sediment was transferred to a 500 ml beaker. Water was added up to a height of 10 cm above the base. Stirred well and allowed standing for 8 minutes and 50 seconds. The turbid suspension was poured away.
11. The beaker was again filled up to 10 cm with water; the process was repeated till the suspension was no longer turbid at the end of the required period.
12. The residue was collected dried at 105°C and weighed.
13. Soil type was noted using the soil triangle (Fig.-3.11).

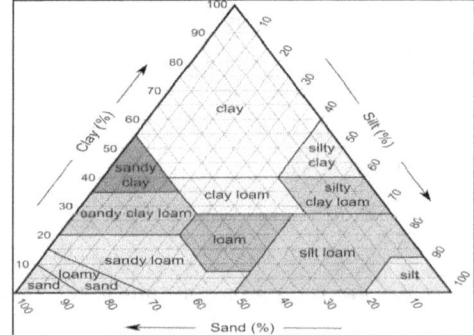

Fig.-3.11: Soil Texture Triangle

Calculation:

$$\text{Coarse Sand (\%)} = \left(\frac{Y - X}{20}\right) \times 100$$

Materials and Methods

Where, 20 g = weight of soil

X g = weight of soil

Y g = weight of soil + dry sand

(Y-X) g = weight of coarse sand

$$\text{Silt and Clay (\%)} = \frac{(Y - X)}{(20 \times 25) \times 1000} \times 100$$

Where, 25 ml = volume of suspension

20 g = weight of soil,

X g = weight of dish

Y g = weight of dish + silt + clay

(Y-X) g = weight of silt and clay

$$\text{Clay (\%)} = \frac{(Y - X)}{(20 \times 25) \times 1000} \times 100$$

Where, 20 g = weight of soil

X g = weight of dish

Y g = weight of dish + clay in 25ml suspension

(Y-X) g = weight of clay

$$\text{Fine Sand (\%)} = \left(\frac{Y - X}{20}\right) \times 100$$

Where, 20 g = weight of soil

X g = weight of dish

Y g = weight of dish + fine sand

(Y-X) g = weight of fine sand

3.3.4. pH (Power of Hydrogen)

The soil pH is the negative logarithm of the active hydrogen ion (H^+) concentration in the soil solution. It is the measure of soil sodicity, acidity, or neutrality. It is a simple but very important estimation for soils, since soil pH influences to a great extent the availability of nutrients to crops. It also affects the microbial population in soils. Most nutrient elements are available in the pH range of 5.5 to 6.5. Soil samples collected directly from the moist field condition considered to

Materials and Methods

be most suitable for the existing soil-biological environment studies. Air-dried soil samples are the most commonly used for analysis, estimation, and evaluation perhaps the convenient standard procedure. In various chemical estimations, pH regulation is critical. Specific colors as observed in the presence of various pH indicators and the color changes due to pH change are shown in Annexure-1.2. The procedure for the measurement of soil pH is given below.

Requirements: pH meter with a range of 0-14 pH, Pipette/dispenser, Beaker, Glass rod, Buffer solutions of pH 4, 7, and 9, Calcium chloride solution (0.01M)

Procedure:

1. The pH meter was calibrated, using 2 buffer solutions, one was the buffer of neutral pH (7.0) and the other was chosen based on the soil acidity and salinity. The buffer solution was taken in the beaker. Inserted the electrode alternately in the beakers containing 2 buffer solutions and adjusted the pH.

Fig.-3.12: pH Meter

2. 10 g of soil was weighed into a 50 or 100 ml beaker, added 20 ml of $CaCl_2$ solution (water was used instead of $CaCl_2$ solution throughout the procedure because it was used as a suspension medium).

3. The soil was allowed to absorb $CaCl_2$ solution without stirring, and then thoroughly stirred for 10 seconds using a glass rod.

4. The suspension was stirred for 30 minutes and recorded the pH on calibrated pH meter (Fig.-3.12). The soil-based on pH value due to reactions has been shown in Annexure-1.6.

3.3.5. Electrical Conductivity (EC)

Electrical conductivity (EC) is a measure of the ionic transport in a solution between the anode and cathode. This means the EC is normally considered to be a measurement of the dissolved salts in a solution. Like a metallic conductor, they obey Ohm's law. Since the EC depends on the number of ions in the solution, it is important to know the soil/water ratio used. The EC of soil is conventionally based on the measurement of the EC in the soil solution extract from a saturated soil paste, as it has been found that the ratio of the soil solution in saturated soil paste is approximately two-three times higher than that at field capacity. As the determination of EC of soil solution from a saturated soil paste is cumbersome and demands a 400-500 g soil sample for the determination, a less complex method is normally used. Generally, a 1:2 soil/water suspension is used.

Requirements: EC meter, Beakers (25 ml), Erlenmeyer flasks (250 ml), Pipettes, Filter paper, 0.01M Potassium chloride solution (KCl): This solution gave electrical conductivity of 1411.8×10^{-3} i.e. 1412 mmhos/cm (or 1.412 mS/cm) at 25°C.

Procedure:
1. 40 g of soil sample was taken into 250 ml Erlenmeyer flask, added 80 ml of distilled water, the flask was stoppered and shaken on the reciprocating shaker for an hour.
2. Filtered through Whatman No.1 filter paper and filtrate was used for measurement of conductivity.

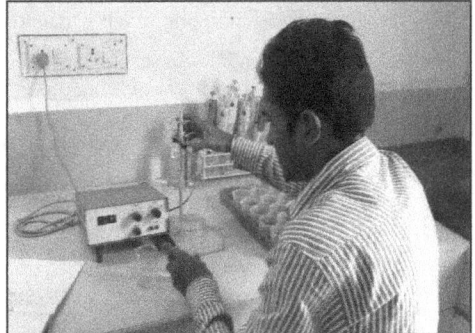
Fig.-3.13: Soil Electrical Conductivity Testing

3. The conductivity electrode was washed with distilled water and rinsed with standard KCl solution.
4. Before the use of the conductivity electrode, it was calibrated with 0.01M KCl solution at 25°C.
5. The electrode was washed and dipped in the soil extract.
6. The digital display was recorded which corrected to 25°C (Fig.-3.13).

Note: Electrical conductivity of the soluble salt content in the extract was measured in mmhos/cm which was an indication of the salinity status of the soil. The conductivity can also be expressed as mS/cm. The general interpretation of EC values has shown in Annexure-1.7.

Materials and Methods

3.3.6. Organic Carbon by Volumetric method (Walkley and Black, 1934)

Organic matter estimation in the soil can be done by different methods. Loss of weight on ignition can be used as a direct measure of the organic matter contained in the soil. It can also be expressed as the content of organic carbon in the soil. It is generally assumed that on average organic matter contains about 58 % organic carbon. Organic carbon/ matter can also be estimated by volumetric and colorimetric methods. However, the use of potassium dichromate ($K_2Cr_2O_7$) involved in these estimations is considered a limitation because of its hazardous nature. Organic carbon is contained in the soil organic fraction, which consists of cells of microorganisms, plant and animal residues at various stages of decomposition, stable humus synthesized from residues, and highly carbonized compounds such as charcoal, graphite, and coal. Soil organic matter content can be used as an index of N availability (potential of a soil to supply N to plants) because the content of N in soil organic matter is relatively constant.

Principle: The organic matter (humus) in the soil gets oxidized by Chromic acid (Potassium dichromate (Cr_2O_7) plus concentrated H_2SO_4) utilizing the heat of dilution of H_2SO_4. The unreacted dichromate is determined by back titration with ferrous (ammonium) sulfate (redox titration).

$$2Cr_2O_7^{2-} + 3C^\circ + 16H^+ = 4Cr^{3+} + 3CO_2 + 8H_2O$$

The amount of $Cr_2O_7^{2-}$ remaining after reaction with soil organic matter is also estimated calorimetrically (intensity of green color) after removal of soil by filtration or centrifugation. Dichromatic methods that use the heat of dilution or minimal; heating do not give complete oxidation of organic compound in the soil although the most active forms of organic carbon converted to CO_2. When Fe^{2+} is present in a higher amount in soil, it will be oxidized to Fe^{3+} by $Cr_2O_7^{2-}$, resulting in a positive error in the most analysis, i.e., giving higher values for organic carbon content.

$$2Cr_2O_7^{2-} + 3C^\circ + 16H^+ = 4Cr^{3+} + 3CO_2 + 8H_2O$$

So, by sufficient air-drying of the soil (about 1 to 2 weeks), Fe^{2+} will be oxidized to Fe^{3+} and organic carbon can be estimated accurately.

Requirements: Conical flask (500ml), Pipettes (2, 10 and 20 ml), Burette (50 ml), analytical balance, Magnetic stirrer, Bubbler, Funnel, Phosphoric acid (85%), Sodium fluoride solution (2%), Sulphuric acid (96%) containing 1.25% Ag_2SO_4, Standard 0.1667 M $K_2Cr_2O_7$, Standard 0.5 M $FeSO_4$ solution, Diphenylamine indicator

Procedure:
1. 1 g of prepared soil sample was weighed in a 500 ml conical flask.
2. 10 ml 0.1667M $K_2Cr_2O_7$ solution was added and 20 ml concentrated H_2SO_4 containing Ag_2SO_4. Excessive swirling was avoided because that would result in organic particles adhering to the sides of the flask out of the solution.
3. It was mixed thoroughly and allowed the reaction to complete for 30 minutes. The flask was placed on an insulation pad during this time to avoid rapid heat loss.
4. The reaction mixture was diluted with 200 ml water and 10 ml H_3PO_4.
5. Then 10 ml of 85 % NaF solution was added and 2 ml of diphenylamine indicator.
6. The solution was titrated with standard 0.5M $FeSO_4$ solution to a brilliant green color (Fig.-3.14).
7. Blank has run without sample simultaneously.

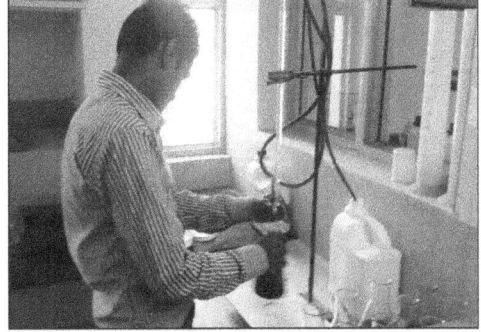

Fig.-3.14: Soil Organic Carbon Testing

Calculation:

$$\text{Organic Carbon (\%)} = \left[10\,(S - T) \times \frac{0.003}{S}\right] \times \left[\frac{100}{\text{Wt. of Soil}}\right]$$

Since one gram of soil was used, this equation simplifies to: $\frac{3\,(S-T)}{S}$

Where, S = ml $FeSO_4$ solution required for blank

T = ml $FeSO_4$ solution required for soil sample

3 = Eq W of C (weight of C is 12, valency is 4, hence Eq W is 12 ÷ 4 = 3.0)

0.003 = weight of C (1000ml 0.1667M $K_2Cr_2O_7$ = 3 g C

3.3.7. Total Nitrogen (Kjeldahl method, 1883)

Total Nitrogen includes all forms of inorganic N, like NH_4, NO_3, and also

Materials and Methods

NH_2 (Urea), and the organic N compounds like proteins, amino acids, and other derivatives. Depending upon the form of N present in a particular sample, a specific method is to be adopted for getting the total nitrogen value. While the organic N materials can be converted into simple inorganic ammoniacal salt by digestion with sulphuric acid, for reducing nitrates into ammoniacal form, the use of salicylic acid or Devarda's alloy is made in the modified Kjeldahl method. At the end of digestion, all organic and inorganic salts are converted into ammonium form which is distilled and estimated by using standard acid. As the precision of the method depends upon the complete conversion of organic N into NH_4-N, the digestion temperature and time, solid: acid ratio and the type of catalyst used has an important bearing on the method. The ideal temperature for digestion is 320° to 370°C. At lower temperatures, the digestion may not be complete, while above 410°C, the loss of NH_3 may occur. The salt: acid (weight: volume) ratio should not be less than 1:1 at the end of digestion. Commonly used catalysts to hasten the digestion process are $CuSO_4$ or Hg. Potassium sulphate is added to raise the boiling point of the acid so that loss of acid by volatilization is prevented.

Principle: It is generally employed for the determination of total-N. It involves two steps: (1) Digestion of sample to convert organic-N to NH^+_4 and (2) Determination of ammonium-N in the digest by distillation. It measures only organic and ammonium forms of nitrogen excluding nitrate nitrogen. Organic and ammonical nitrogen is converted to ammonium sulfate and ammonia gas is distilled into boric acid and titrated with a dilute strong such as hydrochloric acid.

Requirements: Kjeldahl digestion and distillation unit (Fig.-3.15), conical flasks, Burettes, Pipettes, Sulphuric acid-H_2SO_4 (93-98% or sp. gravity 1.84), Copper sulphate - $CuSO_4 \cdot H_2O$ (AR grade), Potassium sulphate or anhydrous sodium sulphate (AR grade), Methyl red indicator, Salicyclic acid for reducing NO_3 to NH_4, Devarda's alloy for reducing NO_3 to NH_4, 35%

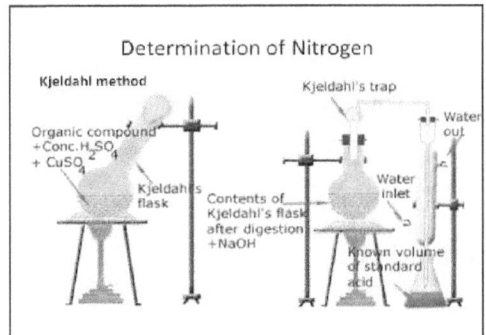

Fig.-3.15: Kjeldahl Nitrogen Determination Method

Materials and Methods

sodium hydroxide solution, 0.1M NaOH, 0.1M HCl or 0.1M H_2SO_4

Procedure:
1. 1 g soil sample was weighed and placed in a Kjeldahl flask.
2. 0.7 g of copper sulphate, 1.5 gm K_2SO_4, and 30 ml H_2SO_4 were added.
3. Heated gently until frothing ceases. To reduce frothing, a small amount of paraffin or glass beads was added.
4. Flask was boiled briskly until the solution was cleared and then continued digestion for at least 30 minutes.
5. Flask was removed from the heater and allowed to cool, added 50 ml water, and transferred to distilling flask.
6. Accurately 20-25 ml standard acid (0.1M H_2SO_4) was taken in the receiving conical flask so that there was at least 5 ml of the acid. 2-3 drops of methyl red indicator were added. Enough water was added to cover the end of the condenser outlet tubes.
7. Added 30 ml of 35 % NaOH in the distilling flask in such a way through the wall of the tube that the contents did not mixed.
8. The contents were heated to evaporate the ammonia for about 30 - 40 minutes.
9. Receiving flask was removed and washed outlet tube into receiving flask with a small amount of distilled water.
10. The excess acid was titrated in the distillate with 0.1M NaOH.
11. Blank was determined on reagents using the same quantity of standard acid in a receiving conical flask.

Calculation:

$$\text{Nitrogen (\%)} = \frac{1.401(V_1 M_1 - V_2 M_2) - (V_3 M_1 - V_4 M_2)}{W \times df}$$

Where, V_1 = ml of standard acid taken in flask for samples
V_2 = ml of standard NaOH used in titration
V_3 = ml of standard acid taken to receiving flask for blank
V_4 = ml of standard NaOH used in titrating blank
M_1 = Molarity of standard acid
M_2 = Molarity of standard NaOH
W = Weight of sample taken (1 g)
df = Dilution factor of sample
(If 1 g for estimation, the df will be 100).

Note: 1000 ml of 0.1 M HCl or 0.1 M H_2SO_4 = 1.401 g Nitrogen

Materials and Methods

Precautions: The material after digestion should not solidify, no NH_4 should be lost during distillation and if the indicator changes color during distillation, the determination must be repeated using either a smaller sample weight or a larger volume of standard acid.

3.3.8. Available Phosphorus (Bray's and Olsen's method)

Two methods are most commonly used for the determination of available phosphorus in soils: Bray's Method No.1 for acidic soils and Olsen's Method for neutral and alkaline soils. In these methods, specific colored compounds are formed with the addition of appropriate reagents in the solution, the intensity of which is proportionate to the concentration of the element being estimated. The color intensity is measured spectrophotometrically. In the spectrophotometric analysis, the light of definite wavelength (not exceeding say 0.1 to 1.0 nm in bandwidth) extending to the ultraviolet region of the spectrum constitutes the light source. The photoelectric cells in the spectrophotometer measure the light transmitted by the solution.

A spectrophotometer, as its name implies, is two instruments in one cabinet - a spectrometer and a photometer. A spectrometer is a device for producing colored light of any selected color (or wavelength) and, when employed as part of a spectrophotometer, is usually termed a monochromator and is generally calibrated in wavelengths (nm). A photometer is a device for measuring the intensity of the light, and when incorporated in a spectrophotometer is used to measure the intensity of the monochromatic beam produced by the associated monochromator. Generally, the photometric measurement is made first with a reference liquid and then with a colored sample contained in similar cells interposed in the light beam: the ratio of the two intensity measurements being a measure of the opacity of the sample at the wavelength of the test. The approximate wavelength ranges of complementary colors are given in Annexure-1.8.

Bray's method no. 1 for acid soil (Bray and Kurtz, 1945)

Principle: This method has been widely used as an index of available P in soil. The combination of HCl and NH_4F is digested to remove easily acid-solution P forms, largely calcium phosphate, and a portion of the aluminum and iron phosphates. The NH_4F dissolves aluminum and iron phosphate by its complexion formation with these

Materials and Methods

metal ions in an acidic solution.

Requirements: Spectrophotometer, Pipette (2, 5, 10 and 20 ml), Beakers/ flasks (25, 50, 100 and 500 ml), Bray Extractant No 1, Molybdate reagent, Stannous chloride solution (Stock Solution), Stannous chloride solution (Working Solution)

Procedure:
1. Preparation of the Standard Curve: 0.1916 g of pure dry KH_2PO_4 was dissolved in 1 liter of distilled water. This solution contained 0.10 mg P_2O_5/ml and was preserved as a standard stock solution of phosphate. Then 10 ml of that solution was diluted to 1 liter with distilled water. Now solution contained 1 µg P_2O_5/ml (0.001 mg P_2O_5/ml). In a separate 25 ml flask; 1, 2, 4, 6, and 10 ml of this solution had taken. 5 ml of the extractant, 5 ml of the molybdate reagent were added to each and diluted with distilled water up to about 20 ml. Added 1 ml of diluted $SnCl_2$ solution, again shook and diluted up to the 25 ml of the mark. After 10 minutes, the blue color of the solution was read in the spectrophotometer at 660 nm wavelength. The absorbance readings were plotted on the graph against µg P_2O_5 values. After that plotted points were joined.
2. Extraction: Added 50 ml of Bray's extractant no. 1 to the 100 ml conical flask containing a 5 g soil sample. The extractant was shaken for 5 minutes and filtered.
3. Development of color: 5 ml of the filtered soil extract was taken with a bulb pipette in a 25 ml measuring flask; 5 ml of the molybdate reagent was delivered with an automatic pipette, diluted to about 20 ml with distilled water, shook, and added 1 ml of the dilute $SnCl_2$ solution with a bulb pipette. Filled to the 25 ml mark and shook thoroughly. Blue color after 10 minutes was read on the spectrophotometer at 660 nm wavelength after setting the instrument to zero with the blank which was prepared similarly but without the soil.

Calculation:

$$\text{Available Phosphorus (kg/ha)} = \left(\frac{A}{1000000}\right) \times \left(\frac{50}{5}\right) \times \left(\frac{2000000}{5}\right) - 4A$$

Where, Weight of the soil taken = 5 g
Volume of the extract = 50 ml
Volume of the extract taken for estimation = 5 ml
Volume made for estimation (dilution = 5 times) = 25 ml
Amount of P observed in the sample on the standard curve = A (µg)
Weight of 1 ha of soil up to a depth of 22 cm is taken as 2 million kg

Materials and Methods

Olsen's Method for alkaline soil (Olsen *et al.*, 1954)

Requirements: Bicarbonate extractant, Activated carbon, Molybdate reagent, and stannous chloride solution

Procedure:

1. Preparation of the standard curve: The procedure was the same as in Bray's method no. 1.
2. Extraction: 50 ml of the bicarbonate extractant was added into a 100 ml conical flask, containing 2.5 g of soil sample and added 1 gm of activated carbon. It was shaken for 30 minutes on the mechanical shaker and then filtered.
3. Development of color: The procedure is the same as described under the Bray's method.

Calculation:

Same as described under the Bray's Method No. 1.

$$\text{Phosphorus (ppm)} = \frac{\text{Phosphorus (kg/ha)}}{5.1296}$$

Caution: Despite all precautions, the intensity of blue color changes slightly with every batch of molybdate reagent. It was imperative to check the standard curve by using 2 or 3 dilutions of the standard phosphate solution. Moreover, the standard curve which was not tallied was drawn again with a fresh molybdate reagent.

3.3.9.   Available Potassium (Flame Photometric method by Toth and Prince, 1949)

Potassium present in the soil is extracted with neutral ammonium acetate of 1 molarity. This is considered as plant-available K in the soils. It is estimated with the help of a flame photometer. This is a well-accepted method.

Requirements: Multiple Dispenser or automatic pipette (25 ml), Flasks and beakers (100 ml), Flame Photometer, Molar neutral ammonium acetate solution, Standard potassium solution, working potassium standard solutions

Procedure:

1. Preparation of the Standard Curve: The flame photometer was set up by atomizing 0 and 20 µg Potassium/ml of solutions alternatively to 0 and 100 reading. Intermediate working standard solutions were atomized and readings were

Materials and Methods

recorded. These readings were plotted against the respective potassium contents and to get a straight line of the standard curve.

2. Extraction: 25 ml of the ammonium acetate extractant was added to a conical flask fixed in a wooden rack containing 5 gm of soil sample. Shook for 5 minutes and filtered.

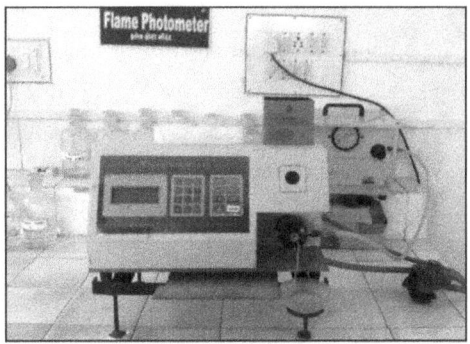

Fig.-3.16: Flame Photometer

3. Potash was determined in the filtrate with the flame photometer (Fig.-3.16).

Calculation:

$$\text{Available Potassium (kg/ha)} = A \times \left(\frac{25}{5}\right) \times \left(\frac{2000000}{1000000}\right) - 10A$$

Where, A = content of K (µg) in the sample, as read from the standard curve

$$\text{Potassium (ppm)} = \frac{\text{Potassium (kg/ha)}}{2.688}$$

3.3.10. Methods for Available Zinc, Copper, Iron and Manganese (Micronutrients)

For estimation of micronutrients also, it is the plant available form which is critical and not the total content. The major objective of a soil test for micronutrients, like macronutrients, is to determine whether soil can supply adequate micronutrients for optimum crop production or whether nutrient deficiencies are expected in crops grown on such soils. The most commonly studied micronutrients are Zn, Cu, Fe, and Mn and the same have been dealt with here. Different extractants have been developed for assessing plant available nutrient (element) content in the soils. The elements so extracted can be estimated quantitatively through chemical methods or instrumental techniques. Commonly used extractants for different elements are given in Annexure-1.9.

Ethylene Damine-Teraacitic Acid (EDTA) + Ammonium Acetate is commonly used for the extraction of many elements. Diethylene Triamine Pentaacetic

Materials and Methods

Acid (DTPA) is yet another common (universal) extractant and is widely used for the simultaneous extraction of elements, like Zn, Cu, Fe, and Mn. This extractant was advanced by Lindsay and Norvell (1978). The estimation of elements in the extract is done with the help of an Atomic Absorption Spectrophotometer (AAS). Critical limits for DTPA extractable micronutrient elements as proposed by Lindsay and Norvell, 1978 are given in Annexure-1.10.

Principle of Extraction: DTPA is an important and widely used chelating agent, which combines with free metal ions in the solution to form soluble complexes of elements. To avoid excessive dissolution of $CaCO_3$, which may release occluded micronutrients that are not available to crops in calcareous soils and may give erroneous results, the extractant is buffered in slightly alkaline pH. TriEthanol Amine (TEA) is used as a buffer because it burns cleanly during atomization of extractant solution while estimating on AAS. The DTPA can complex each of the micronutrient cations as 10 times its atomic weight. The capacity ranges from 550 to 650 mg/kg depending upon the micronutrient cations.

Extracting Solution (DTPA): DTPA 0.005M, 0.01M $CaCl_2\,2H_2O$ and 0.1M TEA extractant:- 1.967 g of DTPA and 13.3 ml of TEA was added in 400 ml distilled water in a 500 ml flask. 1.47 g of $CaCl_2\,2H_2O$ was taken in a separate 1000 ml flask. 500 ml distilled water was added and shook to dissolve. Added DTPA+TEA mixture in $CaCl_2$ solution and made 1 liter of volume. pH was adjusted to 7.3 by using 1M HCl before making the volume.

Principle of Estimation: The extracted elements can be estimated by various methods, which include volumetric analysis, spectrometry, and atomic absorption spectroscopy. Volumetric methods such as EDTA and $KMnO_4$ titrations are used for the estimation of zinc and Mn, and iron, respectively. Copper can be estimated by titration with $Na_2S_2O_3$. Spectrometric methods are deployed in the estimation of specific colors developed due to the presence of an element, which forms a colored compound in the presence of specific chemicals under a definite set of conditions. The color intensity has to be linear with the concentration of the element in question. The interference due to any other element has to be eliminated. Such methods are the dithizone method for estimation of zinc, orthophenonthroline method for iron, potassium periodate method for manganese, carbamate method for copper. The

Materials and Methods

chemical methods are generally cumbersome and time taking. Hence the most commonly employed method is atomic absorption spectrometry. Here, the interference by other elements is almost nil or negligible because the estimation is carried out for an element at a specific emission spectra line. In fact in AAS, traces of one element can be accurately determined in the presence of a high concentration of other elements.

Principle of Atomic Absorption Spectrophotometry (AAS): The procedure is based on flame absorption rather than flame emission and upon the fact that metal atoms absorb strongly at discrete characteristic wavelengths which coincides with the emission spectralines of a particular element. The liquid sample is atomized. The hollow cathode lamp which precedes the atomizer emits the spectrum of the metal used to make the cathode. This beam traverses the flame and is focused on the entrance slit of a monochromator, which is set to read the intensity of the chosen spectral line. Light with this wavelength is absorbed by the metal in the flame and the degree of absorption is the function of the concentration of the metal in the flame, the concentration of the atoms in the dissolved material is determined. For elemental analysis, a working curve or a standard curve is prepared by measuring the signal or absorbance of a series of standards of known concentration of the element underestimation. From such a curve, the concentration of the element in an unknown sample is estimated.

Atomic Absorption Spectroscopy (Fig.-3.17) can be successfully applied for the estimation of Zn, Cu, Fe, and Mn. For specific estimation on AAS, hollow cathode lamps, specific to specific elements are used. The specifications of relevant hollow cathode lamps

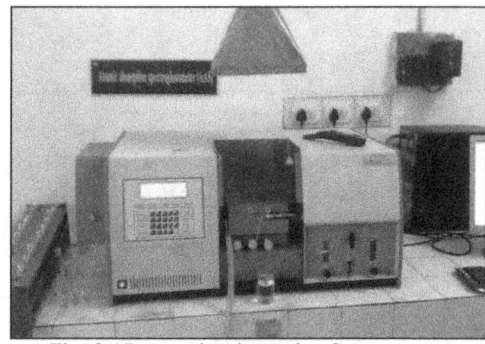

Fig.-3.17: Atomic Absorption Spectrometer

are given in Annexure-1.11. Running parameters that are specific to a particular model are given in the software provided with the equipment manual. Accordingly, the current supply, wavelength of hollow cathode lamp, integration time, and anticipated estimation ranges are fixed. The hollow cathode and Deutorium lamps are required to

Materials and Methods

be properly aligned before starting the equipment. After proper alignment and adjustment, standard curves are prepared to ensure that the concentration of the elements in solutions perfectly relates to the absorbance.

Preparation of standard solutions: Readymade standard solutions 1000 µg/ml or 1 mg/ml (1000 ppm) of dependable accuracy were supplied with the AAS and were also available with the suppliers of chemical reagents. Standard solutions were prepared in the laboratory by metal element foils of 100% purity or standard chemical salts. The quantities of chemicals were required to make 1 liter 100 µg/ml standard solution for different elements which are given in Annexure-1.12. In the case of Zn, Cu, and Fe, 1000 µg/ml (1000 ppm) standard solution was preferably prepared by dissolving 1 g pure metal wire and made to 1-liter volume as per the method described under each element. It was diluted to obtain the required concentration. In the case of Manganese, $MnSO_4 \cdot H_2O$ was preferred.

3.3.10.1. Preparation of standard curves:

a. **Zinc**

Requirements: Standard Zinc Solution, Glass-distilled or demineralized acidified water of pH 2.5 + 0.5, and Working Zn standard solutions.

Procedure:

1. Flaming the solutions: Standards were atomized on atomic absorption spectrophotometer at a wavelength of 213.8 nm (Zn line of the instrument).
2. A standard curve of known concentrations of zinc solution was prepared by plotting the absorbance values on Y-axis against their respective zinc concentration on X-axis.

Precautions: Weighing was done on an electronic balance. All the glass apparatus used were washed first with dilute hydrochloric acid (1:4) and then with distilled water. The pipette was rinsed with the same solution to be measured. The outer surface of the pipette was wiped with filter paper after use. After the use of the pipette, they were placed on clean dry filter paper to prevent contamination.

b. **Copper**

Requirements: Standard copper solution, Glass-distilled or demineralized

Materials and Methods

acidified water of pH 2.5 + 0.5, and Working Cu standard solutions

Procedure:
1. The standards were flamed on an atomic absorption spectrophotometer at a wavelength of 324.8 nm (Cu line of the instrument).
2. The standard curve was prepared with the known concentration of copper on the X-axis by plotting against the absorbance value on the Y-axis.

c. **Iron**

Requirements: Standard iron solution: Glass-distilled or demineralized acidified water of pH 2.5 ± 0.5 and Working Fe standard solutions.

Procedure:
1. The standards were flamed on an atomic absorption spectrophotometer at a wavelength of 248.3 nm (Feline of the instrument).
2. The standard curve was prepared with the known concentration of copper on the X-axis by plotting against the absorbance value on the Y-axis.

d. **Manganese**

Requirements: Standard Mn solution: Glass-distilled or de-mineralized acidified water of pH 2.5 + 0.2 and Working Mn standard solutions.

Procedure:
1. The standards were flamed on an atomic absorption spectrophotometer at a wavelength of 279.5 nm (Mn line of the instrument).
2. The standard curve was prepared with the known concentration of Mn on the X-axis by plotting against the absorbance value on the Y-axis.

Procedure for extraction by DTPA:
1. Once standard curves have been prepared, proceed for extraction by DTPA.
2. 10 g of soil sample was taken in a 100 ml narrow-mouth polypropylene bottle.
3. 20 ml of DTPA was added to extract the solution.
4. The bottle was stoppered and shook for 2 hours at room temperature (25°C).
5. The content using filter paper No.1 or 42 was filtered and the filtrate was collected in polypropylene bottles.
6. Blank was prepared by following all steps except taking a soil sample.

Note: The extract so obtained is used for the estimation of different micronutrients. For extraction of the more accurate quantity of an element that has a higher degree of

Materials and Methods

correlation with plant availability, there are element-specific extractants. An extractant standardized/recommended for a given situation in a country may be used. The estimation procedure on AAS, however, remains unchanged.

Estimation on AAS:
1. An element-specific hollow cathode lamp was selected and mounted on AAS.
2. The flame was started and the instrument was set at zero by using the blank solution.
3. Standard solutions of different concentrations were aspirated one by one and recorded the readings.
4. The standard curve was prepared by plotting the concentration of the element concerned and the corresponding absorbance in different standard samples (as described before).
5. In the inaccurately performed operation, a straight-line relationship was obtained between the concentration of the element and the absorbance on AAS with a correlation coefficient that might nearly as high as 1.0.
6. The soil extractant was not only aspirated but also obtained for estimation of the nutrient element in the given soil sample and the readings were observed.
7. The content of the element in the soil extract was found by observing its concentration on the standard curve against its absorbance.

Calculation:

$$\text{Micronutrient (mg/kg)} = C \mu g \times 2 (\text{dilution factor})$$

Where, Dilution factor = 2 (Soil sample taken = 10 g and DTPA used = 20 ml), X = Absorbance reading on AAS of the soil extract of a particular element, C µg/ml = Concentration of micronutrient as read from the standard curve for the given absorbance (X) and 1 mg/kg = 1 ppm

3.4. Study of Soil Microbiota

Soil contains enormous numbers and kinds of microorganisms. In addition to the multitudes of bacteria, there are protozoans, yeasts, molds, algae, and microscopic worms in unbelievable numbers. With ideal temperature and moisture conditions, soil provides excellent culture media for many kinds of microorganisms. This is especially true of cultivated and improved soils. In many different ways, these

Materials and Methods

organisms contribute to the fertility of the very medium they inhabit. The action of certain autotrophic protists on minerals produces substances, organic and inorganic, that are available to plants. Maintaining a proper balance of available nitrogen to photosynthetic plants is one of the most important activities of some forms of bacteria. The decomposition of lifeless plant and animal tissues returns materials to soils in a form that is reusable by plants. No scientific experiment would produce the desired result unless and until it is properly carried out. Each technique in this chapter is described in sufficient detail to enable satisfactory results to be obtained; however, certain techniques will require practice before the expertization is achieved. The instructions which were recommended for each technique was followed carefully and understood before the practical work was carried out because of the following reasons:

1. Risk of Contamination: The atmosphere contains a dense microbial population. When handling microorganisms, there is a constant danger of contamination from the air. Such contamination is most likely to occur when the techniques are faulty. Therefore, the object of aseptic techniques is to expose the cultures as little as possible to any risk of contamination.
2. Risk of Infection: The need for standard techniques to be followed becomes even more important when dealing with pathogenic organisms. Unless and until the aseptic techniques are strictly followed there is a constant risk of infection for all the individuals working in the laboratory.
3. Fluctuations in Results: Any experiment designed should have reproducibility. For most of the experiments, the experimental procedures should remain standard throughout. Should these conditions fluctuate, the results would not be reliable.
4. Speed and Economy: To minimize the wastage of time and materials, it is essential to follow the standard procedures and acquaint oneself thoroughly with the basic microbe handling techniques.

3.4.1. Aseptic Technique

Aseptic transfer of a culture from one culture vessel to another is successful only if no contaminating microorganisms were introduced in the process. A transfer might involve the transport of organisms from an isolated colony on a plate of solid medium to a broth tube, or inoculating various media (solid or liquid) from a

Materials and Methods

broth culture for various types of tests. The general procedure is as follows:

1. **Work Area Disinfection:** The work area was first treated with a disinfectant to kill any microorganisms that might be present. This step destroys vegetative cells and viruses; endospores, however, are not destroyed in this brief application of a disinfectant.
2. **Wire loop and Needle:** The transport of organisms will be performed with an inoculating loop or needle. To sterilize the loop or needle before picking up the organisms, heat must be applied with a Bunsen burner flame, rendering them glowing red-hot.
3. **Culture Tube Flaming:** Before inserting the cooling loop or needle into a tube of culture, the tube cap was removed and the mouth of the culture tube was flamed. Once the organisms had been removed from the tube, the tube mouth must be flamed again before returning the cap to the tube.
4. **Liquid Medium Inoculation:** If a tube of the liquid medium is to be inoculated, the tube mouth must be flamed before inserting the loop into the tube. To disperse the organisms on the loop, the loop should be twisted back and forth in the medium. If an inoculating needle is used for stabbing a solid medium, the needle is inserted deep into the medium.
5. **Final Flaming:** Once the inoculation is completed, the loop or needle is removed from the tube, flamed as before, and returned to a receptacle. These tools should never be placed on the tabletop. The inoculated tube is also flamed before placing the cap on the tube.
6. **Petri Plate Inoculation:** To inoculate a Petri plate, no heat was applied to the plate and a loop was used for the transfer. When streaking the surface of the medium, the cover should be held diagonally over the plate bottom to prevent air contamination of the medium.
7. **Final Disinfection:** When all work was finished, the work area was treated with disinfectant to ensure that any microorganisms deposited during any of the procedures were eliminated.

3.4.2. Standard Plate Count (SPC) or CFU of Soil Sample

It is a quantitative bacteriological analysis that enumerates the total viable

Materials and Methods

population, capable of growing under a given set of conditions. The actual numbers are probably greatly underestimated by this method. Several limitations of this technique are: No single nutrient medium or growth conditions can meet the entire nutrient and other requirements of soil microorganisms. For example, i) anaerobes fail to grow in aerobic conditions, ii) autotrophs do not multiply in an organic medium, iii) many organisms like cellulose utilizers, nitrifying bacteria, sulphate reducers, etc. fail to grow or grow poorly on nutrient agar medium. Thus counts represent only a fraction of the total viable bacterial population of the soil.

Principle: SPC is based on the assumption that each viable bacterium develops into a distinct colony. Hence, an original number of microorganisms in the sample can be calculated from the number of colonies and then multiplying with dilution factor.

Requirements: Soil sample, Sterile distilled water dilution tubes (4.5 or 9.0 ml and 10 ml), sterile melted nutrient agar tubes, sterile petri dishes, and sterile 1ml pipettes

Procedure:

1. With a sterile spatula (flame sterilized after dipping in alcohol) 1 g soil sample was weighed on a sterile paper.
2. The soil sample was transferred to a sterile 9 ml dilution blank (this gave the 10^{-1} dilution of the soil sample).
3. Contents of the tubes were mixed vigorously and allowed soil particles to settle.
4. Prepared 10^{-2}, 10^{-3}, 10^{-4}..... dilutions of the soil supernatant (3.4.2.2.: Preparation Serial Dilution).
5. From each dilution, a fixed amount (approximately 0.2 ml) was transferred into a sterile melted nutrient ager tube which is previously cooled to 50°C (3.4.2.1: Preparation of Nutrient Medium), mixed well, and immediately poured in sterile petri dishes.
6. Plates (e.g. as $10^{-1}/0.2$ or as the case may be) were labeled, clearly indicating the dilution and the volume plated respectively.
7. All plates were incubated at

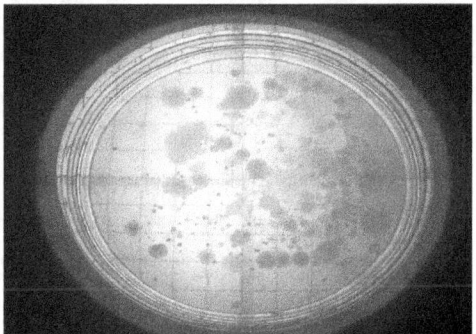

Fig.-3.18: Colony Forming Unit count on Colony Counter

Materials and Methods

37 °C for 24 hours.

8. Total numbers of colonies were counted which developed on each plate. Colony counter can be used to help to count colonies (Fig.-3.18: Colony Forming Unit count on Colony Counter).
9. The final number of organisms was calculated which present in the soil as follows. Note: An alternative method for inoculation can be used to transfer the aliquots directly into a sterile plat followed by pouring melted nutrient agar on it and mixing it well before it solidifies.

Calculation and interpretation of results:

1. For accuracy of results, countable plates that have colonies in between 30-300. Fewer than 30 colonies are not acceptable for statistical reasons, and more than 300 colonies on a plate are likely to produce colonies too close to each other to be distinguished as individual CFUs (colony forming units).
2. Lower dilutions (e.g. 10^{-1}, 10^{-2}) at times may show confluent (lawn) growth, due to the high load of organisms in the sample, these results are represented as "too numerous to count" (TNTC).
3. Final CFUs/ ml can be calculated by multiplying the average number of colonies per countable plate by the reciprocal of the dilution and the reciprocal of the volume plated.

$$\text{Colony Forming Units/ml} = \frac{\text{Average number of colonies} \times \text{Dilution}}{\text{Volume plated on agar plate}}$$

3.4.2.1. Preparation of Nutrient Medium

The nutrient broth has been one of the earliest media which used in bacteriology. It is a basal medium that supports the growth of a wide range of nutritionally undemanding chemoorganotrophic bacteria. Such a medium may be supplemented with particular nutrients or growth factors (to support the growth of nutritionally fastidious organisms); or with selectively inhibitory sub-stances (to prevent the growth of unwanted organisms).

Requirements: Meat extract, Beef extract, peptone, NaCl, distilled water, pH paper or pH meter, flask, measuring cylinder, digital balance, beaker, bunsen burner, tripod, and hot plate

Materials and Methods

Procedure: Preparation of Nutrient Broth

1. 0.3 g of meat extract, 1 g of peptone, and 0.5 g NaCl were weighted.
2. The above ingredients were mixed in the flask and added about 90 ml of distilled water; contents were mixed well.
3. The flask was placed in a boiling water bath till the ingredients get dissolved.
4. The flask was allowed to cool and measured the initial pH either by pH paper or by pH comparator.
5. Adjusted pH to 7.6 using either dilute acid or alkali.
6. The final volume was adjusted to 100 ml with distilled water.
7. The broth was distributed and so prepared, in tubes or the flask as desired.
8. Sterilized by autoclaving at 121°C temperature and 15 lbs pressure for 15 minutes.
9. The medium was allowed to cool and used.

Procedure: Preparation of Nutrient Agar

1. The nutrient agar was prepared which is described above up to step No. 6.
2. 2.5 g of agar was weighed and added to the broth prepared as described above.
3. The flask was placed in a boiling water bath till the agar gets dissolved.
4. The pH of the medium was rechecked (adjust it if necessary).
5. Slants were prepared by distributing the medium in tubes.
6. Sterilized by autoclaving at 121°C temperature and 15 lbs pressure for 15 minutes.
7. After sterilization, the tubes were placed in a slanting position and allowed to cool without disturbance till it solidifies.
8. For desired plates, the sterilized medium was kept in a flask and distributed in plates.
9. Before pouring the sterile medium into a sterile petri dish, the medium should be cooled down to 50 - 55°C, to minimize moisture deposition on the lid of the petri dish.
10. About 20 ml of the medium was poured aseptically into sterile petri dishes and the plates were placed on the horizontal surface and allowed to cool (Fig.-3.19).

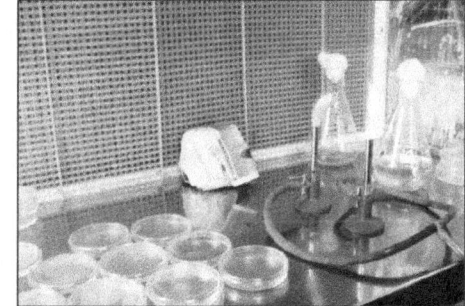

Fig.-3.19: Preparation of Nutrient Agar Plates

Materials and Methods

3.4.2.2. Preparation Serial Dilution

This is the method by which the concentration of a particular substance was diluted in a stepwise manner. This technique of serial dilution is normally used in Assay (quantitative estimation) of certain compounds like sugars, proteins using certain standard techniques; Assay of bacteriophages; Serological reactions where the determination of titer is essential; and Bacteria, under good growing conditions, will multiply into such large population that it is often necessary to dilute them to isolate single colonies or to obtain estimates of their numbers.

Procedure:

1. This procedure is based on using a 1/10 stock (e.g. Soil Extract of 1 g with diluent added to 10 ml).
2. Four screw-capped tubes were labeled as actual stock, 10^{-2}, 10^{-3} and 10^{-4}.
3. 9 ml aliquot of sterile water was pipetted into each tube by using a sterile pipette.
4. By using a new sterile 10 ml pipette, a 1 ml aliquot of full strength stock was pipetted in the first tube and capped.
5. It was mixed for few seconds; the tube was vigorously flicked to adequately disperse the bacteria evenly throughout the tube and broken up bacterial clumps. The test tube was not shaken! That has given the actual stock dilution of the sample.
6. With a sterile 100ml micropipette, 1 ml aliquot of actual stock was transferred in the second tube and mixed well.
7. This second tube now had a 1:100 (10^{-2}) dilution of the original broth culture. There were still way too many bacteria in here to count if you were to plate them, so further dilution was necessary.
8. Using a new sterile tip, 1 ml was transferred from the second tube (1:100 or 10^{-2}) and added into the third tube labeled 1:1000 or 10^{-3}.
9. Repeated the tube mixing procedure to get 10^{-6}, 10^{-7}.

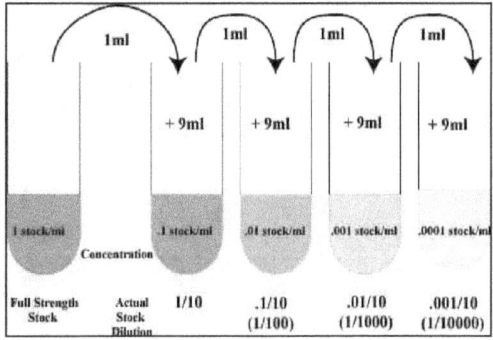

Source: Google

Fig.-3.20: Preparation of Serial Dilution

Materials and Methods

and 10^{-8} for the agricultural soil (Fig.-3.20).

3.4.3. Isolation and Pure Culturing (NFB, PSB, and KSB)

In the study of bacterial flora from the soil, water, food, or any other part of our environment that results in the mixed bacteria populations. The occurrence of a single species is very rare. For the specific culture study, morphological as well as biochemical characteristics of an individual species are essential and that microorganisms must have in pure culture. Several different methods for the pure culture of microorganisms are available. The two most frequently used methods are streak plate and pour plate. Both plate techniques involve thinning the organisms so that the individual species can be selected from the others. In the current study, special/ selective media were used. Ashby's Mannitol Agar for Nitrogen-fixing bacteria, Pikovskayas Agar for Phosphate solubilizing bacteria, and Aleksandrow Agar for Potassium solubilizing bacteria were used. The selected soil sample was serially diluted to minimize the overcrowded growth of bacteria. The streak plate method was used for isolation and pure culturing.

3.4.3.1. Media Preparation

3.4.3.1.1 Preparation of Ashby's Mannitol Agar for Nitrogen Fixing Bacteria

The agar medium is used for the cultivation of Azotobacter species that can use mannitol and atmospheric nitrogen as a source of carbon and nitrogen respectively.

Requirements: Ashby's Mannitol Agar, flask, measuring cylinder, digital balance, beaker, bunsen burner, tripod, and hot plate

Procedure:
1. 40.7 g of Ashby's Mannitol Agar was weighed and suspended in 1000 ml distilled water (Annexure-2 list).
2. Medium ingredients were properly melted by applying just boiling heat.
3. The medium was sterilized by autoclaving at 121°C temperature and 15 lbs pressure for 15 minutes.
4. After sterilization and before pouring the sterile medium into a sterile petri dish, the medium should be cooled down to 50 - 55°C, to minimize moisture deposition on the lid of the petri dish.

Materials and Methods

5. About 20 ml of the medium was poured aseptically into sterile petri dishes and the plates were placed on the horizontal surface and allowed to cool.
6. Soil supernatant was serially diluted (10^{-6}, 10^{-7} and 10^{-8}) and 0.1 ml of suspension was spread on the surface of the agar medium.
7. The plates were incubated at $28\pm1°C$ for 5 - 7 days and the colonies were observed.

3.4.3.1.2 Preparation of Pikovskayas Agar for Phosphate Solubilizing Bacteria

The agar medium is recommended for the detection of phosphate solubilizing soil microorganisms.

Requirements: Pikovskayas Agar, flask, measuring cylinder, digital balance, beaker, bunsen burner, tripod, and hot plate

Procedure:
1. 31.3 g of Pikovskayas Agar was weighed and suspended in 1000 ml distilled water (Annexure-2 list).
2. Medium ingredients were properly melted by applying just boiling heat.
3. The medium was sterilized by autoclaving at $121°C$ temperature and 15 lbs pressure for 15 minutes.
4. After sterilization and before pouring the sterile medium into a sterile petri dish, the medium should be cooled down to 50 - $55°C$, to minimize moisture deposition on the lid of the petri dish.
5. About 20 ml of the medium was poured aseptically into sterile petri dishes and the plates were placed on the horizontal surface and allowed to cool.
6. Soil supernatant was serially diluted (10^{-6}, 10^{-7} and 10^{-8}) and 0.1 ml of suspension was spread on the surface of the agar medium.
7. The inoculated plates were incubated at $28\pm1°C$ for 3–5 days; the colonies exhibiting clear zones of solubilization were selected.

3.4.3.1.3 Preparation of Aleksandrow Agar for Potassium Solubilizing Bacteria

Aleksandrow Agar is used for the isolation and detection of Potassium solubilizing bacteria from soil samples.

Requirements: Aleksandrow Agar, flask, measuring cylinder, digital balance, beaker, bunsen burner, tripod, and hot plate

Materials and Methods

Procedure:

1. 29.60 g of Aleksandrow Agar was weighed and suspended in 1000 ml distilled water (Annexure-2 list).
2. Medium ingredients were properly melted by applying just boiling heat.
3. The medium was sterilized by autoclaving at 121°C temperature and 15 lbs pressure for 15 minutes.
4. After sterilization and before pouring the sterile medium into a sterile petri dish, the medium should be cooled down to 45 - 50°C, to minimize moisture deposition on the lid of the petri dish.
5. About 20 ml of the medium was poured aseptically into sterile petri dishes and the plates were placed on the horizontal surface and allowed to cool.
6. Soil supernatant was serially diluted (10^{-6}, 10^{-7} and 10^{-8}) and 0.1 ml of suspension was spread on the surface of the agar medium.
7. The inoculated plates were incubated at 28±1°C for 3–5 days; the colonies exhibiting clear zones of solubilization were selected.

3.4.4. Probable Identification of Unknown Bacteria

In the identification of unknown bacteria, the cultural and biochemical characteristics of bacteria were important to know/ understand. The first step in the identification procedure, the information was accumulated that pertains to the organisms' morphological, cultural, and biochemical characteristics. This step was followed by probable identification using taxonomic keys and Bergey's Manual of Systematic Bacteriology.

3.4.4.1 Morphological Study

In this study, morphological characteristics of an unknown bacterial organism have been learned as much as possible. Whether the organism was rod-, coccus-, or spiral-shaped; whether or not it was pleomorphic; gram staining reaction; and the presence or absence of endospores. All this morphological information has provided a starting point in the categorization of an unknown. Morphology of the unknown has been understood by the motility test and gram-staining, in which how the organism was arranged, what was the shape and size, motile or not, and gram reaction as well.

Materials and Methods

3.4.4.1.1 Motility Determination

When attempting to identify an unknown bacterium it is usually necessary to determine whether the microorganism is motile. For non-pathogens, two slide techniques and a tube method for pathogens can be used. Each method has its advantages and limitations. A discussion of each procedure follows.

The wet mount slide: When working with non-pathogens, the simplest way to determine motility is to place a few loopful of the organism on a clean slide and cover it with a cover glass. In addition to being able to determine the presence or absence of motility, this method is useful in determining cellular shape (rod, coccus, or spiral) and arrangement (irregular clusters, packets, pairs, or long chains). A wet mount is especially useful if phase optics has used.

The hanging drop slide: If it is necessary to study viable organisms on a microscope slide for a longer time than is possible with a wet mount, one can resort to a hanging drop slide. As shown in (Fig.-3.21: The Hanging drop slide of Motility test) organisms were observed in a drop that was suspended under a cover glass in a concave depression slide. Since the drop lies within an enclosed glass chamber, drying out occurs very slowly.

Tube Method: When working with pathogenic microorganisms such as the typhoid bacillus, it is too dangerous to attempt to determine motility with slide techniques. A much safer method is to culture the organisms in a special medium that can demonstrate the presence of motility. The procedure is to inoculate a tube of semisolid or SIM medium that can demonstrate the presence of motility. Both media have a very soft consistency that allows motile bacteria to migrate readily through them causing cloudiness.

Requirements: Microscope, slides, cover glasses, depression slide, tubes of semisolid or SIM medium, cultures of microorganisms, inoculating loop, needle, bunsen burner

Procedure for Hanging Drop Slides: According to (Fig.-3.21) hanging drop slides was prepared for each organism. Clean cover glasses were used and each slide was labeled with a china marking pencil. When a loopful of organisms placed on the cover glass, the loop was flamed. After placing the slide on the microscope, the steps written below were followed:

Materials and Methods

1. The slide was examined first in the low-power objective. To get a clear focus, the coarse adjustment knob was used. The greater thickness of the depression slide can prevent one from being able to focus at the stop point.
2. Once the image was visualized under low power, the high-dry objective was swung into the position and readjusted the lighting. Most of the bacteria have drawn to the edge of the drop by surface tension, so focused on the edge of the drop.

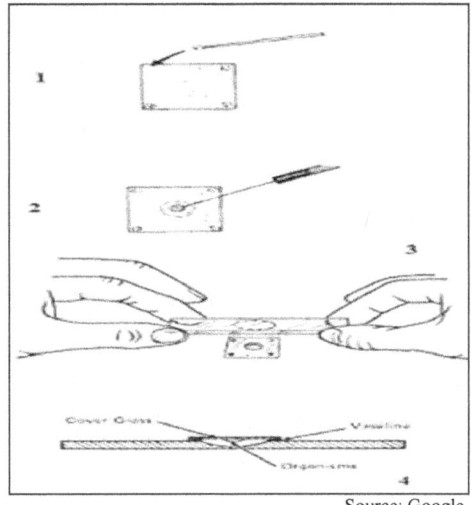

Source: Google
Fig.-3.21: The Hanging Drop Slide of Motility Test

3. Oil immersion lense can also be used.
4. This setup was done faster. The water of condensation may develop to decrease clarity and the organisms become less motile with time.

Procedure for Tube Method: Organisms were inoculated in tubes according to the following instructions:

1. Tubes of semisolid media were labeled and placed initials.
2. The inoculating needle was flamed and cooled, and inserted into the culture after flaming the neck of the tube.
3. Cap from the tube of the medium was removed; flamed the neck and stabbed 2/3 of the way down to the bottom, as shown in Image plate-6: ab. The neck of the tube was flamed again before returning the cap to the tube.
4. Steps 2 and 3 were repeated for the other culture.
5. Tubes were incubated at room temperature for 24 to 48 hours.
6. The next day tubes were observed and results were noted.

3.4.4.1.2   Gram Staining

In 1884 the Danish bacteriologist Christian Gram developed a staining technique that separates bacteria into two groups: those that are gram-positive and those that are gram-negative. The procedure is based on the ability of microorganisms to retain the purple color of crystal violet during decolorization with alcohol. Gram-negative bacteria are decolorized by the alcohol, losing the purple color of crystal violet. Gram-positive bacteria are not decolorized and remain purple. After decolorization, safranin, a red counterstain, is used to impart a pink color to the decolorized gram-negative organisms.

Principle: Gram-positive bacteria have a thick mesh-like cell wall that is made up of peptidoglycan (50 - 90 % of the cell wall), which stains purple. Peptidoglycan is mainly a polysaccharide composed of two subunits called N-acetyl glucosamine and N-acetyl muramic acid. As adjacent layers of peptidoglycan are formed, they are cross-linked by short chains of peptides utilizing a transpeptidase enzyme, resulting in the shape and rigidity of the cell wall. The thick peptidoglycan layer of Gram-positive organisms allows these organisms to retain the crystal violet-iodine complex and stains the cells as purple. Gram-negative bacteria have a thinner layer of peptidoglycan (10% of the cell wall) and lose the crystal violet-iodine complex during decolorization with the alcohol rinse, but retain the counterstain Safranin, thus appearing reddish or pink. They also have an additional outer membrane that contains lipids, which is separated from the cell wall by means of periplasmic space.

Requirements: Slides with heat-fixed smears, Gram-staining kit, and wash bottle, bibulous paper, bacterial culture

Procedure:

1. The bacterial smear on the glass slide was prepared by heat fixing. Then crystal violet was applied for 20 seconds.
2. The stain was washed off briefly with a wash bottle of distilled water and drained off excess water.
3. The smear was covered with Gram's iodine solution and left for one minute on a stand.
4. Gram's iodine was poured off and the smear was flooded with 95% ethyl alcohol for 10 to 20 seconds for this critical step of decolorization by checking the colorless flow of solvent. Thick smears were required more time.
5. The action of the alcohol was stopped by rinsing the slide with water from the wash bottle for a few seconds.

Materials and Methods

6. Now the smear was covered with Safranin for 20 seconds (Some technicians prefer more time here).
7. The slide was washed gently for few seconds, blot dried with bibulous paper, and air-dried.
8. The slide was examined under oil immersion and noted results.

3.4.4.1.3 Cultural Characteristics

The cultural characteristics of an organism pertain to its macroscopic appearance on different kinds of media. Descriptive terms used in the study are given in Table-3.1.

Colour	by reflected or transmitted light: fluorescent, iridescent, opalescent
Consistency	butyrous, mucoid, friable, membranous
Edge	entire, undulate, lobate, crenated, erose, fimbriate, curled, effuse
Elevation	effuse, raised, low convex, convex or dome-shaped, umbonate, with or without bevelled margin
Emulsifiable	easy or difficult, forms homogeneous or granular suspension or remains membranous when mixed in a drop of water
Form	filiform, spreading, rhizoid
Opacity	transparent, translucent, opaque
Shape	circular, irregular, radiate, rhizoid
Size	diameter in millimeters
Structure	amorphous, granular, filamentous, curled
Surface	smooth, rough (fine, medium, or coarsely granular), ringed, papillate, dull or glistening, heaped up, dry or moist

Table-3.1: Terms used in Colonial Morphology

3.4.4.2 Biochemical Study/Characteristics

3.4.4.2.1 Durham Tube Sugar Fermentations

When Durham tubes containing various sugars bank use, we can determine what sugars an organism can ferment. If an organism can ferment a particular sugar, the acid will be produced and gas may be produced. The presence of acid is detectable with the color change of a pH indicator in the medium. Gas production is revealed by the formation of a void in the inverted vial of the Durham tube. The sugar broths used here contain 0.5 % of the specific carbohydrate plus sufficient amounts of beef extract and peptone to satisfy the nitrogen and mineral needs of most bacteria. The pH indicator phenol red is included for acid detection. This indicator is red when the pH is above 7 and yellow below this point. Although there are many sugars that one might be, glucose, lactose, and mannitol are logical ones, to begin with.

Requirements: Durham tubes with phenol red indicator, glucose broth, lactose broth, mannitol broth, isolated bacterial culture

Procedure:

1. 3 or 4 drops of phenol red indicator were added into control tubes of glucose, lactose, and menitol broth, which were inoculated with unknown bacterial culture and incubated at optimum temperature 37°C.
2. The control was examined and observed that the phenol red was turned into yellow which was indicating acid production. A gas bubble was also observed in the inverted vial. These observations showed that organisms have fermented glucose to produce acid and gas.
3. Sugar broths in which unknown bacterial culture was inoculated were observed and results recorded.

3.4.4.2.2 Mixed Acid Fermentation (Methyl-Red Test)

A considerable number of gram-negative intestinal bacteria can be differentiated based on the end-products produced when they ferment the glucose in the MR-VP medium. Genera of bacteria such as *Escherichia, Salmonella, Proteus,* and *Aeromonas* ferment glucose to produce large amounts of lactic, acetic, succinic, and formic acids, plus CO_2, H_2, and ethanol. The accumulation of these acids lowers the pH of the medium to 5.0 and less. If methyl red is added to such a culture in which the indicator turns red that indicates the organism is a mixed acid fermenter. These organisms are generally great gas producers, too, because they produce the enzyme formic hydrogenylase, which splits formic acid into equal parts of CO_2 and H_2.

$$HCHOOH \xrightarrow{\text{formic hydrogenylase}} CO_2 + H_2$$

MR-VP medium is essentially a glucose broth with some buffered peptone and dipotassium phosphate. Perform the methyl-red test first on the control tube and then on the unknown.

Requirements: Dropping bottle of methyl-red indicator, isolated bacterial culture

Procedure:

1. 3 or 4 drops of methyl red were added to control and immediately red color in a tube has illustrated the positive methyl-red test.

Materials and Methods

2. The same procedure was repeated for unknown bacterial cultures. In the negative methyl-red test, the unknown bacterial culture became yellow.

3.4.4.2.3 Butanediol Fermentation (Voges-Proskauer Test)

A negative methyl-red test may indicate that the organism being tested produced a lot of 2, 3 butanediol, and ethanol instead of acids. All species of *Enterobacter* and *Serratia,* as well as some species of *Erwinia, Bacillus,* and *Aeromonas,* do just that. The production of these nonacid end-products results in less lowering of the pH in the MR-VP medium, causing the methyl-red test to be negative. Unfortunately, there is no satisfactory test for 2, 3 butanediol; however, acetoin (acetylmethylcarbinol), a precursor of 2, 3 butanediol, is easily detected with Barritt's reagent. Barritt's reagent consists of alpha naphthol and KOH. When added to a 3 to a 5-day culture of MR-VP medium, and allowed to stand for some time, the medium changes to pink or red in the presence of acetoin. Since acetoin and 2, 3 butanediol are always simultaneously present, the test is valid. This indirect method of testing for 2, 3 butanediol is called the Voges-Proskauer test. Perform the Voges-Proskauer test on unknown and test-control tubes of MR-VP medium.

Requirements: Barritt's reagents, 2 pipettes (1ml size), 2 empty test tubes, isolated bacterial culture

Procedure:

1. One empty test tube was labeled for unknown bacterial culture.
2. 1 ml of unknown bacterial culture was pipetted into the empty unknown tube. Separate pipettes have used for each tube.
3. About 0.5 ml (18 drops) of Barritt's solution A was added to each of the tubes that contained 1 ml of unknown bacterial culture.
4. An equal amount of Barritt's solution B was added to the same tubes and incubated at optimum temperature 37°C.
5. The tubes were shaken vigorously every 20 seconds until the tube turned into pink or red color. Then tubes were allowed to stand for 1 or 2 hours for red color development. Vigorous shaking was very important to achieve complete aeration. A positive Voges-Proskauer reaction was pink or red.

3.4.4.2.4 Catalase Production

Most aerobes and facultative that utilize oxygen produce hydrogen peroxide, which is toxic to their enzyme systems. Their survival in the presence of this antimetabolite is possible because they produce an enzyme called *catalase,* which converts the hydrogen peroxide to water and oxygen:

$$2H_2O_2 \xrightarrow{catalase} 2H_2O + O_2$$

It has been postulated that the death of strict anaerobes in the presence of oxygen may be due to the suicidal act of H_2O_2 (hydrogen peroxide) production in the absence of catalase production. The presence or absence of catalase production is an important means of differentiation between certain groups of bacteria. To determine whether or not catalase is produced, it is necessary is to add/place a few drops of 3% H_2O_2 (Hydrogen peroxide) on the slant culture of organisms. If the hydrogen peroxide effervesces, the organism is catalase-positive.

Requirements: 3 % H_2O_2, Isolated bacterial culture

Procedure:

1. While holding a test-unknown tube at an angle, few drops of H_2O_2 were allowed to flow slowly down over the slant. The patterns of bubbles that emerged from the organisms were noted.
2. The test was repeated for other cultures and recorded the observations.

3.4.4.2.5   Oxidase Production

The production of oxidase is one of the most significant tests we have for differentiating certain groups of bacteria. For example, all the *Enterobacteriaceae* are oxidase-negative and most species of *Pseudomonas* are oxidase-positive. Another important group, the *Neisseria,* is oxidase producers. The filter paper method is used here which requires only a loopful of organisms from the plate.

Requirements: TSA (Trypticase Soy Agar) plate was streaked with isolated bacteria, Oxidase test reagents, Whatman no. 2 filter paper

Procedure:

1. Several drops of oxidase test reagent were placed on a piece of Whatman no. 2 filter paper in a petri dish.
2. Loopful of the organisms was removed from one of the colonies and made smear of the organisms over a small area of the paper.

Materials and Methods

3. The positive test has shown violet to purple color change within 10-30 seconds while the negative test has shown light-pink or absence of coloration.
4. Colour change was observed and recorded.

3.4.4.2.6 Nitrate Reduction

Many facultative bacteria can use the oxygen in nitrate as a hydrogen acceptor in anaerobic respiration, thus converting nitrate to nitrite. This enzymatic reaction is controlled by an inducible enzyme called nitratase. The chemical reaction for this enzymatic reaction is as follows:

$$NO_3^- + 2e^- + 2H^+ \xrightarrow{\text{nitratase}} NO_2^- + H_2O$$

Since the presence of free oxygen prevents nitrate reduction, actively multiplying organisms will use up the oxygen first and then utilize the nitrate. In culturing some organisms, it is desirable to use anaerobic methods to ensure nitrate reduction. The nitrate broth used in this test consists of beef extract, peptone, and potassium nitrate. To test for nitrite after incubation, we use two reagents designated as A (sulfanilic acid) and B (dimethyl-alpha-naphthylamine). In the presence of nitrite, these reagents cause the culture to turn red. Negative results must be confirmed as negative with zinc dust.

Requirements: Nitrate broth cultures of unknown bacteria, nitrite test reagents (solutions A and B) zinc dust

Procedure:

1. Isolated unknown bacteria was inoculated in Nitrate broth and incubated at optimal temperature 37°C.
2. 2 or 3 drops of nitrite test solution A and B were added in incubated nitrate broth.
   A red color appeared almost immediately that has indicated a reduction of nitrate.

Caution: Avoided Skin contact with solution-B (Dimethyl-alpha-naphthylamine) which is carcinogenic.

3. The test procedure was repeated for other unknown bacterial. For the negative nitrate reduction test, unknown organisms have not shown red color. All negative results were confirmed as being negative as follows.

Negative Confirmation: A pinch of zinc dust was added to the tube and vigorously shook. The tube which has shown red color was confirmed as being negative.

Materials and Methods

3.4.4.2.7 Starch Hydrolysis

Since many bacteria are capable of hydrolyzing starch, this test has fairly wide application. The starch molecule is a large one consisting of two constituents: amylose, a straight-chain polymer of 200 to 300 glucose units, and amylopectin, a larger branched polymer with phosphate groups. Bacteria that hydrolyze starch produce amylases that yield molecules of maltose, glucose, and dextrin.

Requirements: Starch agar culture plate, Iodine solution (Gram's) is an indicator of starch, isolated bacterial culture

Procedure:

1. Starch agar plates were labeled and streaked. Straight-line streaking has made on each plate and incubated at optimum temperature 37°C.
2. The next day iodine solution was applied to the plate and allowed it to react.
3. When iodine came in contact with a medium containing starch, it turned blue. For hydrolyzed starch or in the absence of starch, the medium has shown/given a clear zone surrounding the growth.
4. By pouring Gram's iodine over the growth on the medium, it has been seen where starch has been hydrolyzed. Moreover, the production of amylase has shown immediately clear adjacent to the growth.
5. Enough iodine was poured over each streak to completely wet the entire surface of the plate. Rotated and tilted the plate gently to spread the iodine.
6. The unknown bacterial culture was observed, compared with the positive result, and recorded.

3.4.4.2.8 Tryptophan Hydrolysis (Indole)

Certain bacteria, such as *E.coli*, can split the amino acid tryptophan into indole and pyruvic acid. The enzyme that causes this hydrolysis is tryptophanase. Indole can be easily detected with Kovacs' reagent. This test is particularly useful in differentiating *E. coli* from some closely related enteric bacteria. Tryptone broth (1%) is used for this test because it contains a great deal of tryptophan. Tryptone is a peptone derived from casein by pancreatic digestion.

Requirements: Kovacs' reagent, tryptone broth cultures of isolated bacteria

Materials and Methods

Procedure:
1. Tube of tryptone broth was labeled which was inoculated with unknown bacterial culture.
2. Tube of tryptone broth was incubated at the optimum temperature 37°C.
3. For the indole test, 10 or 12 drops of Kovacs' reagent were added to culture in tryptone broth. The formation of a red layer at the top of the culture has indicated a positive test.
4. The test was repeated and observed to record the results.

3.4.4.2.9 Urea Hydrolysis

The differentiation of gram-negative enteric bacteria is greatly helped if one can demonstrate that the unknown can produce urease. This enzyme 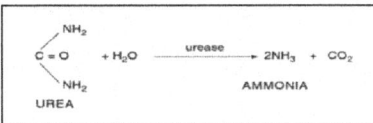 splits off ammonia from the urea molecule, as shown nearby. Urea broth is a buffered solution of yeast extract and urea. It also contains phenol red as a pH indicator. Since urea is unstable and breaks down in the autoclave at 15 psi steam pressure, it is usually sterilized by filtration. It is tubed in small amounts to hasten the visibility of the reaction.

Requirements: urea broths, isolated bacterial culture

Procedure:
1. Tube of urea broth was labeled and inoculated with unknown bacterial culture.
2. The urea broth tube was incubated at the optimum temperature 37°C.
3. Production of urease by an organism in this medium has raised the pH with ammonia. Due to that high pH, the phenol red has changed from a yellow color (pH 6.8) to a red or cerise color (pH 8.1 or more).
4. Urea broth of unknown culture was examined and recorded the results.

3.4.4.2.10 Hydrogen Sulfide (H_2S) Production

Certain bacteria, such as *Proteus vulgaris*, produce hydrogen sulfide from the amino acid cysteine. These organisms produce the enzyme cysteine desulfurase, which works in conjunction with the coenzyme pyridoxyl phosphate. The production of H_2S is the initial step in the deamination of cysteine as indicated in the below

Materials and Methods

reaction: Kligler's iron agar medium is used here to detect hydrogen sulfide production. Media contain iron salts that react with H_2S to form a dark precipitate of iron sulfide.

Requirements: Kligler's iron agar deep, isolated bacterial culture

Procedure:

1. One tube of Kligler's iron agar was labeled for unknown bacterial culture and inoculated by stabbing with a straight wire.

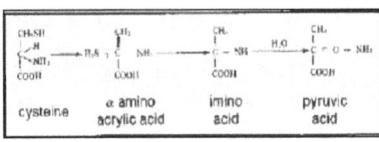

2. The tube was incubated at its optimum temperature 37°C.
3. Kligler's iron agar also contains glucose, lactose, and phenol red. When this medium was used by organisms in a slant that has indicated the excellent medium in the detection of glucose and lactose fermentation.
4. The tube was examined, the formation of black precipitation has indicated a positive test which was recorded as the results.

3.4.4.2.11 Citrate Utilization

The ability of some organisms, such as *E. aerogenes* and *Salmonella typhimurium,* to utilize citrate as a sole source of carbon can be a very useful differentiation characteristic in working with intestinal bacteria. Koser's citrate medium and Simmons citrate agar are two media that are used to detect this ability in bacteria. In both of these synthetic media sodium citrate is the sole carbon source; nitrogen is supplied by ammonium salts instead of amino acids.

Requirements: Simmons citrate agar slant, isolated bacterial culture

Procedure:

1. Tube of Simmons citrate agar was labeled for unknown bacterial culture. A straight wire was used to streak-stab (both) slant; i.e., the slant was streaked first, and then stabbed into the middle of the slant.
2. Incubated at their optimum temperature 37°C.
3. The slant of the medium was examined that inoculated with culture. The distinct Prussian blue color change was noted for positive tests and recorded the results.

3.4.4.2.12 Litmus Milk Reactions

Litmus milk contains 10 % powdered skim milk and a small amount of litmus as a pH indicator. When the medium is made up, its pH is adjusted to 6.8. It is an excellent growth medium for many organisms and can be very helpful in unknown characterization. In addition to revealing the presence or absence of fermentation, it can detect certain proteolytic characteristics in bacteria. A number of facultative bacteria with strong reducing powers can utilize litmus as an alternative electron acceptor to render it colorless.

Requirements: Litmus milk medium, isolated bacterial culture

Procedure:
1. With a loop, a tube of litmus milk medium was inoculated with unknown bacterial culture.
2. Incubated at their optimum temperature 37°C.
3. Since some of the reactions have taken 4 to 5 days to occur, the unknown isolated bacterial culture was incubated for at least this period and examined every 24 hours for the following reactions:

Acid Reaction: Pink litmus has indicated typical fermentative bacteria.

Alkaline Reaction: Blue or purple litmus has indicated many proteolytic bacteria which cause this reaction in the first 24 hours.

Litmus Reduction: White color medium culture has indicated actively reproducing bacteria which reduces the oxidation/reduction potential of the medium.

Coagulation: Curd formation has indicated solidification due to protein coagulation. A tilting tube at 45°C has indicated whether or not this has occurred.

Peptonization: Translucent medium has indicated proteolytic bacteria.

Ropiness: Thick, slimy residue in the bottom of the tube has considered as ropiness which can be demonstrated by a sterile loop. Results of unknown bacterial cultures were recorded.

3.4.5. Cultivation or Preparation of Microbial Inoculums for Amendment

3.4.5.1 Cultivation NFB Inoculum (Riswana, 2016)

A loopfull of Azotobacter pure culture was transferred into a 250 ml Erlenmeyer flask containing 100 ml of Ashby's broth and incubated at 28±2°C on a 120 rpm rotary shaker for 72 hours. After incubation, 10 ml of the inoculums were transferred to 1000 ml of respective broth and kept in a shaking incubator for mass multiplication. The culture was mixed with the carrier material. The carrier material

Materials and Methods

keeps the bacterial strain viable and active for a long duration. 750 ml was mixed thoroughly with 1000 gm of each sterile carrier (Charcoal), adjusted the moisture content to 75 % water holding capacity, packed in polyethylene bags, sealed, and incubated under room temperature. The inoculums were repacked in sterile polyethylene bags and stored at room temperature for further usage.

3.4.5.2   Cultivation PSB Inoculum (Mondal, 2017)

A loopfull of an isolated pure culture of PSB was transferred into a 250 ml Erlenmeyer flask containing 100 ml of Pikovskaya's broth and incubated at $28\pm2°C$ on 120 rpm rotary shaker for a week. After incubation, 10 ml of the inoculums were transferred to 1000 ml of respective broth and kept in a shaking incubator for mass multiplication. The culture was mixed with the carrier material. The carrier material keeps the bacterial strain viable and active for a long duration. In this experiment, cow dung is used as a carrier material. The ratio of Biofertilizer and carrier material was kept at 1:1. Cow dung was used as a carrier. The mixture was packed in polyethylene bags, sealed, and kept for storage at $4°C$ overnight for further usage.

3.4.5.3   Cultivation KSB Inoculum (Priyanka and Sindhu, 2013)

A loopfull of an isolated pure culture of KSB was transferred into a 250 ml Erlenmeyer flask containing 100 ml of Aleksandrov broth and incubated at $28\pm2°C$ on 120 rpm rotary shaker for 10 days. After incubation, 10 ml of the inoculums were transferred to 1000 ml of respective broth and kept in a shaking incubator for mass multiplication. 750 ml was mixed thoroughly with 1000 gm of each sterile carrier (Charcoal), adjusted the moisture content to 75 % water holding capacity, packed in polyethylene bags, sealed, and incubated under room temperature. The inoculums were repacked in sterile polyethylene bags and stored at room temperature for further usage.

3.5.   **Molecular Study of Bacterial Isolates**

3.5.1.   **16s rRNA Partial Sequencing**

Two isolates, NFB and PSB were grown on their respective media. At the edge of the petri plates, colonies were taken by sterile loop and resuspended in 200 µl of Tris-EDTA buffer (10mM Tris-HCl and 1mM EDTA) in an Eppendorf tube. The extracted DNA was run on agarose gel for checking the purity. The mixtures were

Materials and Methods

frozen at -70°C and thawed by boiling at 94°C for 10 minutes. After 10 minutes of centrifugation at 8,000 rpm, the DNA in the supernatant was collected and used as the DNA template for PCR. The 16S ribosomal DNA sequences of bacterial isolates were amplified using universal primers (27 forward and 1492 reverse for NFB gene, 518 forward and 800 reverse for PSB gene). Sequencing of the PCR-amplified products was conducted using primers: 27F includes 20 unique sequences ('5-AGA GTT TGA TCC TGG CTC AG-3') and 1492R includes 22 unique sequences ('5-TACGGYTACCTTGTTACGACTT-3'), 518F includes 20 unique sequences ('5-CCA GCA GCC GCG GTA ATA CG-3') and 800R includes 18 unique sequences ('5-TAC CAG GGT ATC TAA TCC-3') ('5-AAA CTC AAA GGA ATT GAC GG-3'), 685R ('5-TCT ACG CAT TTC ACC GCT AC-3') and 1492R ('5-TAC GGY TAC CTT GTT ACG ACT T-3') on an automated AVI-310 Genetic analyzer (Chromous Biotech Pvt. Ltd., Bangalore).

The obtained two 16S rRNA nucleotide sequences (970 bp and 1171 bp) were deposited at the National Center for Biotechnology Information (NCBI) GenBank database under accession number MT656171 and MT656254. Closely related homologes were identified by comparing the partial 16S rRNA sequence with sequences deposited in the GenBank database by BLAST analysis (www.ncbi.nlm.nih.gov). The 16S rRNA gene partial sequences of strain DPN and DPP were aligned with other nucleotide sequences and the phylogenic tree for both the strains was observed. The hypervariable nucleic acid region of both isolates was compared with closely related sequences.

3.5.2. Phylogenetic Analysis

A straightforward phylogenetic analysis consists of four steps: the first is Alignment (both building the data model and extracting a phylogenetic dataset), the second is determining the substitution model, the third is tree building and the fourth is tree evaluation. When performing a phylogenetic analysis, it often insightful to build trees based on different modifications of the alignment to see how the alignment proposed influences the resulting tree. Phylogenetic sequence data usually consist of multiple sequence alignments; the individual, aligned-base positions are commonly referred to as "sites." These sites are equivalent to "characters" in theoretical phylogenetic discussions, and the actual base (or gap) occupying a site is the "character state". The sequence so obtained was taken up for running NCBI BLAST against nonredundant nucleotide database using megablast algorithm for getting homologous sequences (Johnson *et al.*, 2008).

3.6. Amendment of Microbial Culture and Soil Fertility Assessment

• Microbial cultures of Nitrogen-fixing, Phosphate solubilizing, and Potassium solubilizing bacteria were used for the soil amendment. These were used with the carrier and applied into selected two agricultural fields of the Mehsana District and one field of Narmada District. For the amendment study, 1 m^2 (1m × 1m) square of agricultural land was used for the bacterial inoculum insertion.

• The soil was analyzed after the 3 days of amendment. This analysis was continued for the next 10 days and 25 days of intervals. Soil quality or fertility parameters were analyzed and compared with the previous results for the selected fields.

• Effect of amended isolates on the Castor farm of Mehsana and Sugarcane farm of Narmada district were studied and observed with plant growth and productivity for soil revitalization or rejuvenation.

3.7. Statistical Analyses

Data were analyzed with the aid of IBM SPSS, OriginPro, and MS Excel software packages. Descriptive statistics, Mean comparison with One-Sample T-Test, and Correlation tests were performed for all the soil parameters of the Mehsana and Narmada districts, and both the district data were compared with the Independent Sample Test (T-Test). Descriptive Statistics can be used to determine measures of central tendency (mean) and measures of dispersion (range, standard deviation, minimum and maximum). The mean comparison was done with the One-Sample T-Test for the significance of the data based on the Significance (2-tailed) value. Bivariate Correlations was performed to find inter-correlations of soil parameters based on Pearson's Correlation and Significance (2-tailed) values.

Chapter 4
Result and Discussion

Result and Discussion

4.0 Result and Discussion

Soil is important for all life over the earth. So it is necessary to analyze soil not only to understand its importance but also for its improvement. Now it is evident that the adequate conditions of the soil, is decreasing day by day which is detrimental for biodiversity. This will lead to the improper output/outcome of soil either for forest needs or for agricultural needs. Here, agricultural land soil analysis was done concerning physical, chemical, and microbiological parameters of Mehsana and Narmada districts. The obtained data were statistically analyzed with different software tools. Furthermore, all soil Physico-chemical and microbiological (CFU count) analysis data is represented graphically for both districts. In the microbial study, morphological and biochemical tests were performed for isolated N-fixing and P and K solubilizing microorganisms. They were amended in fields with carriers and further studied for soil quality change.

4.1. Soil Physico-Chemical Assessment and CFUs Result

The data relating to Physico-Chemical Assessment and Colony Forming Units of soil collected from Mehsana and Narmada districts are presented in different tables and discussed soil parameter-wise as under.

4.1.1. Moisture (%)

Data related to soil Moisture of the Mehsana District (Graph-4.1) and Narmada District (Graph-4.2) has been presented in Table-4.1 and Table-4.2 respectively. In the Mehsana District, the maximum soil moisture was 51.26% and the minimum was 4.31%; 51.56% soil moisture was the maximum and 14.19% was the minimum for the Narmada District. Soil moisture content was recorded in good numbers for both the district that may be due to the regular irrigation of agricultural soil.

Sample no	Moisture	Sample no	Moisture	Sample no	Moisture	Sample no	Moisture
1	7.76	26	7.01	51	5.45	76	23.93
2	8.63	27	19.43	52	7.02	77	23.99
3	9.87	28	8.18	53	8.45	78	25.74
4	6.17	29	5.06	54	7.31	79	20.53
5	5.24	30	5.93	55	8.37	80	20.64
6	6.26	31	13.42	56	8.40	81	24.30

Result and Discussion

7	10.82	32	9.29	57	9.39	82	22.88
8	11.45	33	7.60	58	12.15	83	28.21
9	9.71	34	10.38	59	5.99	84	18.40
10	11.09	35	7.27	60	20.70	85	27.13
11	10.06	36	8.79	61	16.23	86	26.97
12	11.43	37	22.71	62	14.09	87	20.79
13	11.65	38	10.34	63	17.99	88	14.46
14	8.18	39	6.80	64	26.01	89	25.42
15	9.05	40	6.17	65	21.91	90	15.57
16	7.65	41	5.52	66	24.70	91	18.77
17	51.26	42	5.82	67	22.12	92	14.48
18	11.24	43	5.82	68	24.69	93	18.43
19	15.53	44	5.78	69	21.18	94	23.98
20	11.74	45	6.79	70	21.21	95	24.29
21	10.25	46	6.82	71	14.97	96	22.01
22	6.39	47	6.62	72	13.55	97	14.22
23	5.40	48	8.03	73	16.85	98	18.18
24	7.62	49	4.31	74	25.20	99	17.77
25	6.59	50	5.44	75	21.36	100	21.11

Table-4.1: Soil Moisture Analysis of Mehsana District

Sample no	Moisture	Sample no	Moisture	Sample no	Moisture	Sample no	Moisture
1	27.63	26	23.31	51	21.20	76	28.85
2	32.59	27	33.94	52	17.79	77	33.49
3	35.26	28	20.69	53	23.61	78	37.33
4	34.52	29	23.82	54	19.78	79	33.89
5	30.79	30	22.50	55	22.25	80	30.94
6	27.15	31	26.44	56	27.71	81	18.98
7	28.37	32	22.55	57	17.12	82	27.71
8	20.29	33	31.10	58	14.19	83	29.79
9	25.28	34	28.68	59	19.33	84	29.42
10	24.92	35	26.15	60	16.09	85	39.28
11	23.49	36	26.14	61	40.39	86	27.65
12	31.58	37	19.60	62	27.32	87	37.80
13	40.55	38	21.20	63	23.73	88	37.25
14	32.36	39	24.53	64	41.76	89	29.00
15	29.33	40	24.39	65	49.30	90	31.96
16	30.21	41	24.09	66	29.74	91	35.34
17	27.78	42	19.63	67	34.07	92	28.35
18	26.07	43	27.94	68	51.56	93	32.10
19	27.28	44	19.36	69	34.97	94	27.23
20	23.90	45	28.95	70	41.54	95	30.75
21	33.78	46	32.64	71	30.48	96	33.80
22	23.47	47	18.27	72	27.75	97	31.13
23	32.63	48	19.99	73	28.27	98	29.96
24	26.55	49	24.24	74	30.84	99	30.36
25	26.30	50	21.64	75	27.58	100	27.34

Table-4.2: Soil Moisture Analysis of Narmada District

Result and Discussion

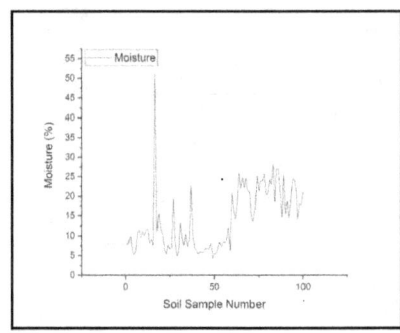 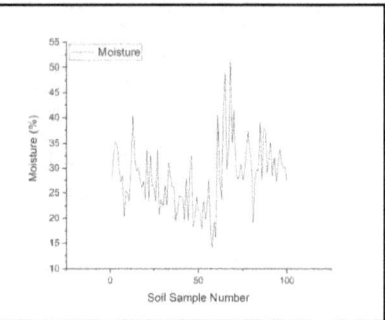

Graph-4.1: Mehsana District soil Moisture   Graph-4.2: Narmada District soil Moisture

4.1.2. Bulk Density (g/cm³)

Data related to soil Bulk Density of the Mehsana District (Graph-4.3) and Narmada District (Graph-4.4) has been presented in Table-4.3 and Table-4.4 respectively. The bulk density of the Mehsana District soil was ranged from 1.222 to 1.592g/cm^3 and the Narmada District soil was ranged from 1.085 to 1.735g/cm^3. The mechanized farming system has to lead to high bulk density in sub-surface soil resulting in compaction, which may not be congenial for crop growth in the long run (Scott *et at.*, 1991).

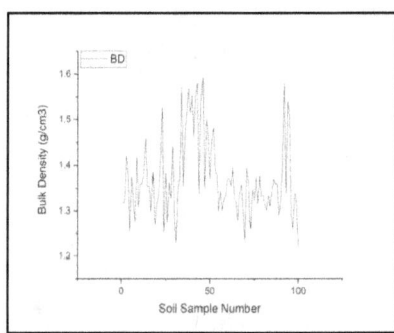 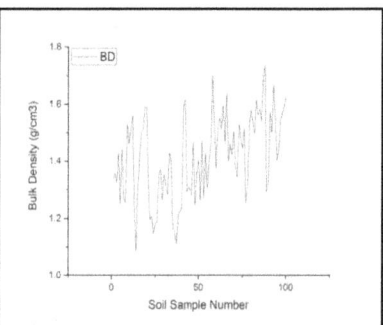

Graph-4.3: Mehsana District soil BD   Graph-4.4: Narmada District soil BD

Sample no	BD	Sample no	BD	Sample no	BD	Sample no	BD
1	1.320	26	1.275	51	1.455	76	1.374
2	1.315	27	1.361	52	1.481	77	1.316
3	1.419	28	1.326	53	1.392	78	1.377
4	1.371	29	1.443	54	1.376	79	1.331
5	1.254	30	1.285	55	1.299	80	1.334
6	1.374	31	1.230	56	1.343	81	1.314

Result and Discussion

7	1.322	32	1.351	57	1.301	82	1.301
8	1.276	33	1.371	58	1.324	83	1.334
9	1.418	34	1.571	59	1.334	84	1.309
10	1.308	35	1.352	60	1.369	85	1.342
11	1.359	36	1.469	61	1.370	86	1.368
12	1.357	37	1.513	62	1.354	87	1.357
13	1.385	38	1.569	63	1.392	88	1.358
14	1.459	39	1.516	64	1.329	89	1.291
15	1.352	40	1.555	65	1.319	90	1.314
16	1.355	41	1.463	66	1.278	91	1.418
17	1.299	42	1.552	67	1.341	92	1.580
18	1.384	43	1.580	68	1.357	93	1.338
19	1.270	44	1.338	69	1.297	94	1.539
20	1.309	45	1.539	70	1.235	95	1.506
21	1.336	46	1.592	71	1.394	96	1.291
22	1.410	47	1.348	72	1.357	97	1.260
23	1.526	48	1.501	73	1.260	98	1.339
24	1.255	49	1.457	74	1.347	99	1.320
25	1.381	50	1.369	75	1.323	100	1.222

Table-4.3: Soil Bulk Density Analysis of Mehsana District

Sample no	BD	Sample no	BD	Sample no	BD	Sample no	BD
1	1.337	26	1.189	51	1.260	76	1.516
2	1.360	27	1.355	52	1.469	77	1.251
3	1.326	28	1.371	53	1.268	78	1.318
4	1.429	29	1.267	54	1.430	79	1.521
5	1.250	30	1.353	55	1.304	80	1.580
6	1.442	31	1.322	56	1.398	81	1.536
7	1.267	32	1.281	57	1.455	82	1.497
8	1.254	33	1.429	58	1.700	83	1.616
9	1.530	34	1.401	59	1.529	84	1.563
10	1.461	35	1.170	60	1.373	85	1.586
11	1.511	36	1.148	61	1.516	86	1.536
12	1.557	37	1.112	62	1.551	87	1.697
13	1.247	38	1.211	63	1.513	88	1.735
14	1.085	39	1.225	64	1.598	89	1.292
15	1.307	40	1.234	65	1.463	90	1.327
16	1.411	41	1.593	66	1.640	91	1.574
17	1.505	42	1.617	67	1.400	92	1.497
18	1.509	43	1.291	68	1.459	93	1.670
19	1.592	44	1.311	69	1.423	94	1.533
20	1.590	45	1.296	70	1.504	95	1.402
21	1.330	46	1.282	71	1.381	96	1.443
22	1.197	47	1.469	72	1.345	97	1.543
23	1.208	48	1.244	73	1.531	98	1.565
24	1.146	49	1.357	74	1.478	99	1.591
25	1.186	50	1.404	75	1.447	100	1.626

Table-4.4: Soil Bulk Density Analysis of Narmada District

4.1.3. Texture

Data related to soil Texture of the Mehsana District (Graph-4.5) and Narmada District (Graph-4.6) has been presented in Table-4.5 and Table-4.6 respectively. In the Mehsana District soil texture, sand was ranged from 45.10 to 88.89% with an average of 76.23%, silt was ranged from 9.26 to 52.94% with an

Result and Discussion

average of 21.91%, and clay was ranged from 1.49 to 5.13% with an average of 2.22%. The Mehsana District soil texture was recorded 78% Loamy Sand, 20% Sandy Loam, 1% Sand, and 1% Loam. In the Narmada District soil texture, sand was ranged from 47.06 to 87.50% with an average of 68.55%, silt was ranged from 10.42 to 50.98% with an average of 29.38%, and clay was ranged from 1.56 to 5.71% with an average of 2.27%. The Narmada District soil texture was recorded 31% Loamy Sand, 68% Sandy Loam and 1% Silt Loam.

Sample no	Sand %	Silt %	Clay %	Soil Type	Sample no	Sand %	Silt %	Clay %	Soil Type
1	79.25	18.87	1.89	Loamy sand	51	74.36	23.08	2.56	Loamy sand
2	80.00	18.18	1.82	Loamy sand	52	66.67	30.95	2.38	Sandy loam
3	77.08	20.83	2.08	Loamy sand	53	81.40	16.28	2.33	Loamy sand
4	73.33	24.44	2.22	Loamy sand	54	73.58	24.53	1.89	Loamy sand
5	65.00	32.50	2.50	Sandy loam	55	84.62	12.82	2.56	Loamy sand
6	75.56	22.22	2.22	Loamy sand	56	72.97	24.32	2.70	Loamy sand
7	74.47	23.40	2.13	Loamy sand	57	78.43	19.61	1.96	Loamy sand
8	75.00	22.50	2.50	Loamy sand	58	86.05	11.63	2.33	Loamy sand
9	76.92	21.15	1.92	Loamy sand	59	79.66	18.64	1.69	Loamy sand
10	74.19	24.19	1.61	Loamy sand	60	79.49	17.95	2.56	Loamy sand
11	71.15	25.00	3.85	Loamy sand	61	83.33	11.90	4.76	Loamy sand
12	88.89	9.26	1.85	Loamy sand	62	80.77	17.31	1.92	Loamy sand
13	70.59	27.45	1.96	Sandy loam	63	84.62	13.46	1.92	Loamy sand
14	69.09	29.09	1.82	Sandy loam	64	73.91	23.91	2.17	Sandy loam
15	82.46	15.79	1.75	Loamy sand	65	45.10	52.94	1.96	loam
16	67.74	30.65	1.61	Sandy loam	66	86.84	11.28	1.88	sand
17	76.74	20.93	2.33	Loamy sand	67	73.91	23.91	2.17	Sandy loam
18	79.07	18.60	2.33	Loamy sand	68	68.29	29.27	2.44	Sandy loam
19	70.00	28.33	1.67	Loamy sand	69	74.36	23.08	2.56	Loamy sand
20	70.18	28.07	1.75	Loamy sand	70	78.26	19.57	2.17	Loamy sand
21	81.82	52.27	2.27	Loamy sand	71	74.55	23.64	1.82	Loamy sand
22	72.34	25.53	2.13	Loamy sand	72	69.81	28.30	1.89	Sandy loam
23	70.00	28.33	1.67	Sandy loam	73	82.98	14.89	2.13	Loamy sand
24	72.73	25.00	2.27	Loamy sand	74	80.85	17.02	2.13	Loamy sand
25	71.64	26.87	1.49	Loamy sand	75	86.27	11.76	1.96	Loamy sand
26	77.27	20.45	2.27	Loamy sand	76	73.68	23.68	2.63	Loamy sand
27	76.47	21.57	1.96	Loamy sand	77	79.49	17.95	2.56	Loamy sand
28	74.24	24.24	1.52	Loamy sand	78	86.27	11.76	1.96	Loamy sand
29	72.09	25.58	2.33	Loamy sand	79	83.72	13.95	2.33	Loamy sand
30	76.74	20.93	2.33	Loamy sand	80	73.81	23.81	2.38	Loamy sand
31	70.45	25.00	4.55	Loamy sand	81	85.37	12.20	2.44	Loamy sand
32	73.08	25.00	1.92	Loamy sand	82	86.05	11.63	2.33	Loamy sand
33	81.48	16.67	1.85	Loamy sand	83	76.74	20.93	2.33	Sandy loam
34	63.64	34.09	2.27	Sandy loam	84	81.13	16.98	1.89	Loamy sand
35	79.55	18.18	2.27	Loamy sand	85	85.00	12.50	2.50	Loamy sand
36	75.00	23.08	1.92	Loamy sand	86	76.92	17.95	5.13	Sandy loam
37	68.52	29.63	1.85	Sandy loam	87	86.27	11.76	1.96	Loamy sand
38	66.67	31.67	1.67	Sandy loam	88	67.86	30.36	1.79	Sandy loam
39	80.49	17.07	2.44	Loamy sand	89	75.56	22.22	2.22	Loamy sand
40	72.34	25.53	2.13	Loamy sand	90	74.14	24.14	1.72	Loamy sand
41	75.44	22.81	1.75	Loamy sand	91	83.33	14.58	2.08	Loamy sand
42	71.43	26.79	1.79	Sandy loam	92	74.47	23.40	2.13	Loamy sand
43	77.55	20.41	2.04	Loamy sand	93	80.39	17.65	1.96	Loamy sand
44	79.55	18.18	2.27	Loamy sand	94	82.35	15.69	1.96	Loamy sand
45	84.00	14.00	2.00	Loamy sand	95	84.00	14.00	2.00	Loamy sand
46	78.57	19.05	2.38	Loamy sand	96	84.31	13.73	1.96	Loamy sand

Result and Discussion

47	82.93	14.63	2.44	Loamy sand	97	61.90	35.71	2.38	Sandy loam
48	69.70	27.27	3.03	Loamy sand	98	72.22	25.00	2.78	Sandy loam
49	78.95	18.42	2.63	Loamy sand	99	63.64	34.09	2.27	Sandy loam
50	72.50	25.00	2.50	Loamy sand	100	79.66	18.64	1.70	Loamy sand

Table-4.5: Soil Texture Analysis of Mehsana District

Sample no	Sand %	Silt %	Clay %	Soil Type	Sample no	Sand %	Silt %	Clay %	Soil Type
1	54.76	42.86	2.38	sandy loam	51	63.79	34.48	1.72	sandy loam
2	80.73	18.55	1.82	loamy sand	52	60.71	37.50	1.79	sandy loam
3	66.67	31.37	1.96	sandy loam	53	82.50	15.00	2.50	loamy sand
4	57.74	40.59	2.09	sandy loam	54	78.57	19.05	2.38	loamy sand
5	84.44	14.22	2.22	loamy sand	55	65.31	32.65	2.04	sandy loam
6	68.24	30.59	1.96	sandy loam	56	55.77	42.31	1.92	sandy loam
7	64.00	35.20	2.00	sandy loam	57	59.57	38.30	2.13	sandy loam
8	70.49	27.87	1.64	sandy loam	58	78.05	19.51	2.44	loamy sand
9	57.71	41.22	1.79	sandy loam	59	47.06	50.98	1.96	silt loam
10	55.77	40.77	3.85	sandy loam	60	54.69	43.75	1.56	sandy loam
11	76.72	21.31	3.28	loamy sand	61	72.41	25.86	1.72	sandy loam
12	80.33	18.03	1.64	loamy sand	62	58.93	39.29	1.79	sandy loam
13	57.69	39.23	3.85	sandy loam	63	61.54	36.54	1.92	sandy loam
14	58.37	38.78	4.08	sandy loam	64	57.41	40.74	1.85	sandy loam
15	62.95	35.97	1.80	sandy loam	65	69.64	28.57	1.79	sandy loam
16	71.38	27.24	1.72	sandy loam	66	64.00	34.00	2.00	sandy loam
17	72.87	34.41	2.02	loamy sand	67	64.58	33.33	2.08	sandy loam
18	62.86	35.51	2.04	sandy loam	68	65.22	32.61	2.17	sandy loam
19	59.07	37.55	4.22	sandy loam	69	66.67	31.25	2.08	sandy loam
20	65.69	32.48	1.82	sandy loam	70	66.67	31.37	1.96	sandy loam
21	62.79	34.88	2.33	sandy loam	71	64.71	33.33	1.96	sandy loam
22	68.89	28.89	2.22	sandy loam	72	60.98	36.59	2.44	sandy loam
23	65.22	32.61	2.17	sandy loam	73	69.39	28.57	2.04	sandy loam
24	57.78	40.00	2.22	sandy loam	74	64.10	33.33	2.56	sandy loam
25	78.85	19.23	1.92	loamy sand	75	68.63	29.41	1.96	sandy loam
26	87.50	10.42	2.08	loamy sand	76	72.00	26.00	2.00	sandy loam
27	82.22	15.56	2.22	loamy sand	77	70.21	27.66	2.13	sandy loam
28	76.19	21.43	2.38	loamy sand	78	70.27	27.03	2.70	sandy loam
29	65.45	32.73	1.82	sandy loam	79	66.67	31.25	2.08	sandy loam
30	68.75	29.17	2.08	sandy loam	80	72.41	25.86	1.72	loamy sand
31	79.07	18.60	2.33	loamy sand	81	70.59	27.45	1.96	sandy loam
32	81.25	16.67	2.08	loamy sand	82	63.83	34.04	2.13	sandy loam
33	75.76	21.21	3.03	loamy sand	83	70.59	27.45	1.96	sandy loam
34	72.50	25.00	2.50	sandy loam	84	70.21	27.66	2.13	sandy loam
35	65.12	32.56	2.33	sandy loam	85	69.05	28.57	2.38	sandy loam
36	61.90	35.71	2.38	sandy loam	86	72.73	22.73	4.55	loamy sand
37	57.69	40.38	1.92	sandy loam	87	70.45	25.00	4.55	sandy loam
38	71.15	26.92	1.92	sandy loam	88	65.91	29.55	4.55	sandy loam
39	73.81	23.81	2.38	sandy loam	89	67.39	30.43	2.17	sandy loam
40	72.34	25.53	2.13	sandy loam	90	77.14	17.14	5.71	loamy sand
41	66.67	31.25	2.08	sandy loam	91	80.00	18.00	2.00	loamy sand
42	61.36	36.36	2.27	sandy loam	92	73.58	24.53	1.89	loamy sand
43	63.83	34.04	2.13	sandy loam	93	86.05	11.63	2.33	loamy sand
44	74.42	23.26	2.33	loamy sand	94	70.45	27.27	2.27	sandy loam
45	74.42	23.26	2.33	loamy sand	95	72.92	25.00	2.08	loamy sand
46	79.07	18.60	2.33	loamy sand	96	74.58	23.73	1.69	loamy sand
47	73.21	25.00	1.79	loamy sand	97	71.70	26.42	1.89	loamy sand
48	56.82	40.91	2.27	sandy loam	98	67.19	31.25	1.56	sandy loam
49	59.65	38.60	1.75	sandy loam	99	72.22	25.93	1.85	loamy sand
50	76.00	22.00	2.00	loamy sand	100	78.05	19.51	2.44	loamy sand

Table-4.6: Soil Texture Analysis of Narmada District

Page | 87

Result and Discussion

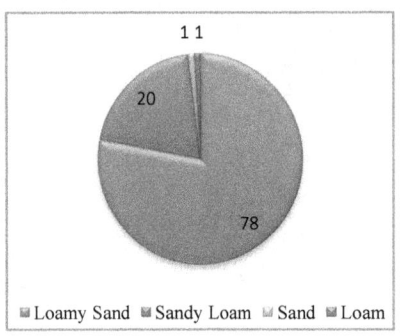 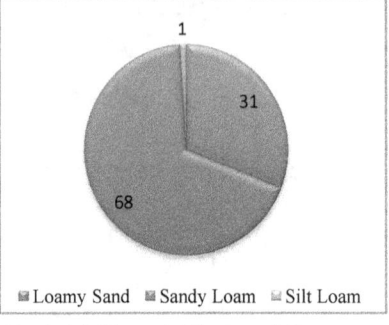

Graph-4.5: Mehsana District soil Texture   Graph-4.6: Narmada District soil Texture

4.1.4.   pH

Data related to soil pH of Mehsana District (Graph-4.7) and Narmada District (Graph-4.8) has been presented in Table-4.7 and Table-4.8 respectively. Mehsana District soil pH varied from 7.24 to 8.50 and Narmada District soil pH varied from 5.93 to 7.43. According to the soil reaction classification of Brady (1985), Mehsana District soil was alkaline (average 7.85 pH) in nature was and Narmada District soil was slightly acidic to neutral (average 6.67 pH). The relative, high pH of the soil might be due to the presence of a high degree, of base saturation. Moreover, the higher pH could be due to an increase in the accumulation of exchangeable sodium and calcium carbonate. The neutral to alkaline pH may be attributed to the reaction of applied fertilizer material with soil colloids, which resulted in the retention of base cations on the exchangeable complex of the soil (Sharma *et al.*, 2008).

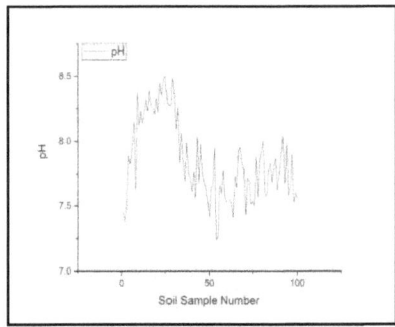 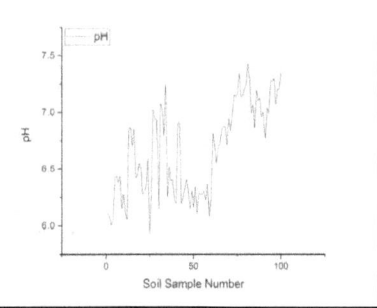

Graph-4.7: Mehsana District soil pH   Graph-4.8: Narmada District soil pH

Result and Discussion

Sample no	pH	Sample no	pH	Sample no	pH	Sample no	pH
1	7.45	26	8.35	51	7.65	76	7.50
2	7.38	27	8.27	52	7.66	77	7.88
3	7.50	28	8.28	53	7.95	78	7.57
4	7.89	29	8.49	54	7.24	79	7.84
5	7.82	30	8.36	55	7.26	80	7.93
6	7.98	31	8.09	56	7.66	81	8.00
7	8.15	32	8.26	57	7.60	82	7.60
8	7.61	33	7.83	58	7.78	83	7.57
9	8.37	34	8.06	59	7.56	84	7.78
10	8.12	35	7.84	60	7.53	85	7.83
11	8.23	36	7.69	61	7.53	86	7.68
12	8.14	37	7.99	62	7.55	87	7.81
13	8.23	38	7.76	63	7.51	88	7.87
14	8.31	39	7.72	64	7.41	89	7.62
15	8.23	40	7.61	65	7.73	90	7.75
16	8.39	41	7.77	66	7.64	91	7.89
17	8.26	42	7.55	67	7.92	92	8.04
18	8.25	43	8.04	68	7.95	93	7.66
19	8.21	44	7.68	69	7.84	94	7.99
20	8.33	45	7.98	70	7.79	95	7.58
21	8.22	46	7.75	71	7.42	96	7.64
22	8.45	47	7.69	72	7.72	97	7.90
23	8.35	48	7.64	73	7.69	98	7.52
24	8.46	49	7.54	74	7.51	99	7.60
25	8.50	50	7.42	75	7.54	100	7.56

Table-4.7: Soil pH Analysis of Mehsana District

Sample no	pH	Sample no	pH	Sample no	pH	Sample no	pH
1	6.11	26	6.25	51	6.35	76	7.35
2	6.07	27	7.02	52	6.11	77	7.14
3	6.00	28	6.95	53	6.28	78	7.15
4	6.05	29	6.93	54	6.28	79	7.20
5	6.43	30	6.15	55	6.27	80	7.25
6	6.44	31	7.08	56	6.30	81	7.43
7	6.38	32	7.02	57	6.22	82	7.30
8	6.44	33	6.80	58	6.37	83	6.99
9	6.15	34	7.25	59	6.08	84	7.07
10	6.28	35	6.25	60	6.25	85	6.86
11	6.12	36	6.52	61	6.82	86	7.20
12	6.05	37	6.40	62	6.70	87	7.10
13	6.85	38	6.41	63	6.55	88	7.13
14	6.87	39	6.23	64	6.70	89	6.96
15	6.70	40	6.20	65	6.72	90	7.00
16	6.86	41	6.90	66	6.86	91	6.77
17	6.42	42	6.91	67	6.87	92	7.04
18	6.45	43	6.20	68	6.88	93	7.00
19	6.55	44	6.25	69	6.71	94	7.28
20	6.51	45	6.33	70	6.94	95	7.27
21	6.28	46	6.41	71	6.84	96	7.30
22	6.30	47	6.30	72	6.97	97	7.07
23	6.35	48	6.15	73	7.15	98	7.20
24	6.60	49	6.31	74	7.14	99	7.20
25	5.93	50	6.16	75	7.16	100	7.35

Table-4.8: Soil pH Analysis of Narmada District

Result and Discussion

4.1.5. Electrical Conductivity (mmhos/cm)

Data related to soil EC of the Mehsana District (Graph-4.9) and Narmada District (Graph-4.10) has been presented in Table-4.9 and Table-4.10 respectively. The EC of the Mehsana District soil ranged from 0.150 to 2.200mmhos/cm and Narmada District soil EC ranged from 0.040 to 0.430mmhos/cm. Based on limits suggested by Muhr *et al.,* (1963), for judging salt problem of soil, average EC was found normal to low (Mehsana district EC 0.348mmhos/cm and Narmada District EC 0.094mmhos/cm) category. The normal EC may be ascribed to the leaching of salts to lower horizons. A similar result was also reported by Sharma *et al.,* (2008).

Sample no	EC	Sample no	EC	Sample no	EC	Sample no	EC
1	0.180	26	0.220	51	0.380	76	0.200
2	0.150	27	0.270	52	2.200	77	0.310
3	0.150	28	0.320	53	0.600	78	0.230
4	0.200	29	0.230	54	0.210	79	0.340
5	0.260	30	0.360	55	0.230	80	0.390
6	0.200	31	0.430	56	0.290	81	0.300
7	0.270	32	0.270	57	0.480	82	0.260
8	0.150	33	0.420	58	0.400	83	0.260
9	0.290	34	0.380	59	0.290	84	0.400
10	0.350	35	0.170	60	0.220	85	0.340
11	0.340	36	0.200	61	0.210	86	0.430
12	0.210	37	0.250	62	0.210	87	0.360
13	0.280	38	0.160	63	0.200	88	0.410
14	0.240	39	0.180	64	0.450	89	0.260
15	0.260	40	0.310	65	0.360	90	0.400
16	0.250	41	0.220	66	0.530	91	0.480
17	0.320	42	0.410	67	0.300	92	0.580
18	0.370	43	0.580	68	0.340	93	0.480
19	0.340	44	0.490	69	0.390	94	0.530
20	0.310	45	0.530	70	0.390	95	0.310
21	1.010	46	0.220	71	0.280	96	0.340
22	0.400	47	0.240	72	0.240	97	0.320
23	0.410	48	0.250	73	0.310	98	0.310
24	0.350	49	0.380	74	0.300	99	0.230
25	0.330	50	0.830	75	0.220	100	0.320

Table-4.9: Soil Electrical Conductivity Analysis of Mehsana District

Sample no	EC	Sample no	EC	Sample no	EC	Sample no	EC
1	0.280	26	0.080	51	0.090	76	0.040
2	0.200	27	0.140	52	0.070	77	0.060
3	0.200	28	0.100	53	0.060	78	0.050
4	0.100	29	0.130	54	0.070	79	0.050
5	0.180	30	0.180	55	0.080	80	0.050
6	0.110	31	0.230	56	0.090	81	0.050
7	0.160	32	0.160	57	0.120	82	0.040
8	0.120	33	0.430	58	0.090	83	0.060
9	0.100	34	0.170	59	0.100	84	0.050
10	0.080	35	0.120	60	0.070	85	0.070
11	0.130	36	0.100	61	0.060	86	0.060

Result and Discussion

12	0.120	37	0.080	62	0.050	87	0.080
13	0.150	38	0.070	63	0.060	88	0.080
14	0.130	39	0.080	64	0.060	89	0.100
15	0.110	40	0.080	65	0.090	90	0.070
16	0.120	41	0.090	66	0.070	91	0.090
17	0.100	42	0.100	67	0.080	92	0.090
18	0.070	43	0.080	68	0.090	93	0.060
19	0.070	44	0.090	69	0.100	94	0.050
20	0.070	45	0.060	70	0.060	95	0.050
21	0.100	46	0.070	71	0.080	96	0.040
22	0.100	47	0.080	72	0.080	97	0.070
23	0.070	48	0.080	73	0.050	98	0.050
24	0.070	49	0.090	74	0.050	99	0.040
25	0.130	50	0.070	75	0.050	100	0.040

Table-4.10: Soil Electrical Conductivity Analysis of Narmada District

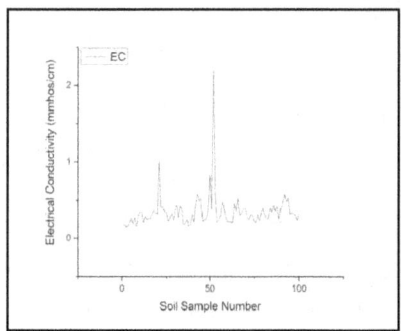 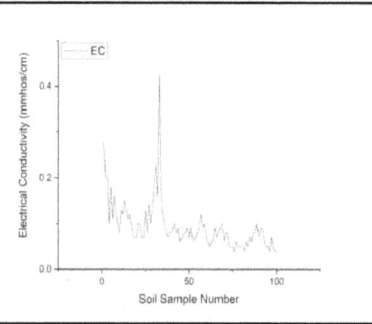

Graph-4.9: Mehsana District soil ECGraph-4.10: Narmada District soil EC

4.1.6. Organic Carbon (%)

Data related to soil Organic Carbon of the Mehsana District (Graph-4.11) and Narmada District (Graph-4.12) has been presented in Table-4.11 and Table-4.12 respectively. In the Mehsana District, the maximum soil OC was 0.950% and the minimum was 0.020%; 4.190% soil OC was the maximum and 0.110% was the minimum for the Narmada District. Based on the limits suggested by Muhr *et al.*, (1963), the average OC (0.407%) of the Mehsana District was low (<0.50%) and the average OC (1.608%) of the Narmada District was High (>0.75%). Variation in organic carbon content is probably due to the differences in agronomic patterns and the use of organic manures in both districts. Low organic carbon in soil may be due to high temperature and good soil aeration which increase the rate of organic matter oxidation. The hydrolysis of organic matter with an increase in pH also plays a role (Talashilkar *et al.*, 2006). And limited biological activity and rapid decomposition of

Result and Discussion

biomass under prevailing climatic conditions (Kadry and Arar, 1975) as well as the poor may the reason for low OC vegetation (Kameriya, 1995).

Sample no	OC	Sample no	OC	Sample no	OC	Sample no	OC
1	0.380	26	0.170	51	0.350	76	0.530
2	0.390	27	0.230	52	0.330	77	0.390
3	0.210	28	0.350	53	0.470	78	0.450
4	0.020	29	0.120	54	0.420	79	0.300
5	0.510	30	0.440	55	0.950	80	0.360
6	0.140	31	0.450	56	0.810	81	0.230
7	0.630	32	0.260	57	0.690	82	0.650
8	0.300	33	0.440	58	0.440	83	0.480
9	0.410	34	0.600	59	0.560	84	0.660
10	0.330	35	0.330	60	0.410	85	0.380
11	0.320	36	0.170	61	0.420	86	0.410
12	0.380	37	0.180	62	0.380	87	0.510
13	0.020	38	0.300	63	0.440	88	0.450
14	0.150	39	0.120	64	0.510	89	0.600
15	0.080	40	0.230	65	0.600	90	0.690
16	0.240	41	0.420	66	0.560	91	0.660
17	0.530	42	0.120	67	0.530	92	0.770
18	0.350	43	0.780	68	0.480	93	0.580
19	0.390	44	0.590	69	0.710	94	0.090
20	0.320	45	0.080	70	0.750	95	0.290
21	0.230	46	0.270	71	0.390	96	0.350
22	0.200	47	0.800	72	0.360	97	0.630
23	0.140	48	0.290	73	0.630	98	0.290
24	0.380	49	0.590	74	0.290	99	0.420
25	0.080	50	0.930	75	0.420	100	0.280

Table-4.11: Soil Organic Carbon Analysis of Mehsana District

Sample no	OC	Sample no	OC	Sample no	OC	Sample no	OC
1	2.480	26	2.250	51	3.780	76	0.660
2	2.630	27	0.460	52	3.920	77	2.750
3	3.710	28	0.340	53	1.830	78	0.710
4	2.430	29	1.070	54	1.610	79	0.470
5	1.940	30	1.490	55	3.670	80	0.680
6	1.130	31	3.120	56	1.010	81	0.570
7	2.630	32	3.300	57	2.130	82	0.710
8	2.390	33	3.830	58	1.490	83	0.200
9	3.220	34	3.980	59	3.790	84	0.930
10	2.170	35	1.730	60	4.190	85	0.560
11	1.850	36	1.160	61	0.750	86	0.110
12	3.140	37	2.560	62	0.900	87	1.050
13	1.600	38	1.840	63	1.020	88	0.720
14	1.130	39	1.940	64	0.450	89	0.960
15	1.590	40	1.770	65	0.830	90	0.410
16	1.390	41	0.920	66	0.600	91	0.750
17	3.380	42	1.450	67	1.020	92	1.050
18	3.380	43	3.100	68	0.620	93	0.120
19	2.450	44	1.750	69	1.200	94	0.240
20	1.410	45	2.420	70	0.530	95	0.560
21	1.690	46	1.550	71	0.450	96	0.950
22	1.640	47	1.710	72	0.290	97	0.270
23	0.680	48	2.810	73	0.530	98	0.930
24	0.990	49	2.560	74	0.600	99	0.110
25	2.500	50	3.050	75	0.690	100	0.720

Table-4.12: Soil Organic Carbon Analysis of Narmada District

Result and Discussion

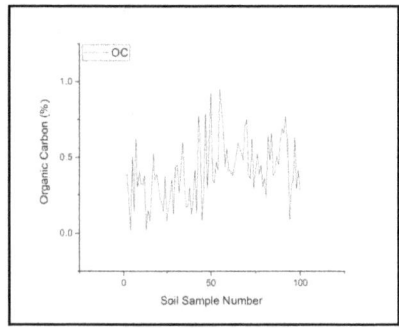
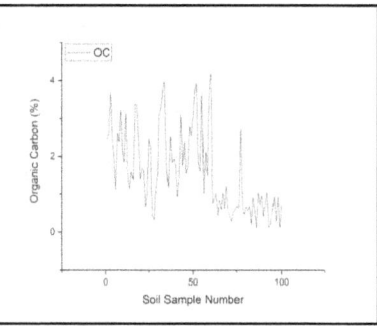

Graph-4.11: Mehsana District soil OC   Graph-4.12: Narmada District soil OC

4.1.7.   Nitrogen (%)

Data related to soil Nitrogen of the Mehsana District (Graph-4.13) and Narmada District (Graph-4.14) has been presented in Table-4.13 and Table-4.14 respectively. In the Mehsana District, the maximum soil Nitrogen was 0.082% and the minimum was 0.002%; and for the Narmada District soil Nitrogen, 0.361% was the maximum and 0.009% was the minimum. Based on the ratings suggested by Subbiah and Asija (1956), N content was low in the Mehsana District and recorded normal to high in the Narmada District. It is quite obvious that the efficiency of applied N is very low because N is lost through various mechanisms like NH_3 volatilization, nitrifications succeeding denitrification, chemical and microbial fixation, leaching, and runoff (Sharma *et al.*, 2008). Low nitrogen status in the soil could be attributed to the low amount of organic carbon soil (Parasuna Rani *et al.*, 1992).

Sample no	N	Sample no	N	Sample no	N	Sample no	N
1	0.033	26	0.015	51	0.030	76	0.046
2	0.034	27	0.020	52	0.028	77	0.034
3	0.018	28	0.030	53	0.041	78	0.039
4	0.002	29	0.010	54	0.036	79	0.026
5	0.044	30	0.038	55	0.082	80	0.031
6	0.012	31	0.039	56	0.070	81	0.020
7	0.054	32	0.022	57	0.059	82	0.056
8	0.026	33	0.038	58	0.038	83	0.041
9	0.035	34	0.052	59	0.048	84	0.057
10	0.028	35	0.028	60	0.035	85	0.033
11	0.028	36	0.015	61	0.036	86	0.035
12	0.033	37	0.016	62	0.033	87	0.044
13	0.002	38	0.026	63	0.038	88	0.039
14	0.013	39	0.010	64	0.044	89	0.052
15	0.007	40	0.020	65	0.052	90	0.059
16	0.021	41	0.036	66	0.048	91	0.057
17	0.046	42	0.010	67	0.046	92	0.066
18	0.030	43	0.067	68	0.041	93	0.050

Result and Discussion

19	0.034	44	0.051	69	0.061	94	0.008
20	0.028	45	0.007	70	0.065	95	0.025
21	0.020	46	0.023	71	0.034	96	0.030
22	0.017	47	0.069	72	0.031	97	0.054
23	0.012	48	0.025	73	0.054	98	0.025
24	0.033	49	0.051	74	0.025	99	0.036
25	0.007	50	0.080	75	0.036	100	0.024

Table-4.13: Soil Nitrogen Analysis of Mehsana District

Sample no	N	Sample no	N	Sample no	N	Sample no	N
1	0.214	26	0.194	51	0.326	76	0.057
2	0.227	27	0.040	52	0.338	77	0.237
3	0.320	28	0.029	53	0.158	78	0.061
4	0.209	29	0.092	54	0.139	79	0.041
5	0.167	30	0.128	55	0.316	80	0.059
6	0.097	31	0.269	56	0.087	81	0.049
7	0.227	32	0.284	57	0.184	82	0.061
8	0.206	33	0.330	58	0.128	83	0.017
9	0.278	34	0.343	59	0.327	84	0.080
10	0.187	35	0.149	60	0.361	85	0.048
11	0.159	36	0.100	61	0.065	86	0.009
12	0.271	37	0.221	62	0.078	87	0.091
13	0.138	38	0.159	63	0.088	88	0.062
14	0.097	39	0.167	64	0.039	89	0.083
15	0.137	40	0.153	65	0.072	90	0.035
16	0.120	41	0.079	66	0.052	91	0.065
17	0.291	42	0.125	67	0.088	92	0.091
18	0.291	43	0.267	68	0.053	93	0.010
19	0.211	44	0.151	69	0.103	94	0.021
20	0.122	45	0.209	70	0.046	95	0.048
21	0.146	46	0.134	71	0.039	96	0.082
22	0.141	47	0.147	72	0.025	97	0.023
23	0.059	48	0.242	73	0.046	98	0.080
24	0.085	49	0.221	74	0.052	99	0.009
25	0.216	50	0.263	75	0.059	100	0.062

Table-4.14: Soil Nitrogen Analysis of Narmada District

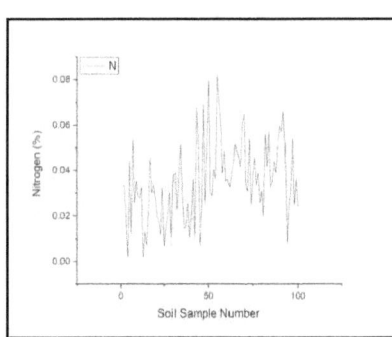 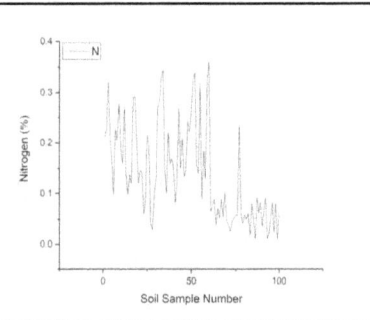

Graph-4.13: Mehsana District soil Nitrogen   Graph-4.14: Narmada District soil Nitrogen

4.1.8. Phosphorous (ppm)

Data related to soil Phosphorous of the Mehsana District (Graph-4.15) and Narmada District (Graph-4.16) has been presented in Table-4.15 and Table-4.16 respectively. In the Mehsana District, the maximum soil P was 10.593ppm and the minimum was 2.889ppm; and 9.747ppm soil P was the maximum and 0.571ppm was the minimum for the Narmada District. Based on the limits suggested by Muhr *et al.,* (1963), the Mehsana District average P (5.564ppm) was normal to low and the Narmada District average P (4.276ppm) was low. This could be attributed to the fixation of released phosphorus by clay minerals and oxides of Fe and Aluminium (Vijay Kumar *et al.,* 1994). The low phosphorus status of soil may be due to low organic carbon content and improper application of phosphate fertilizers. An adequate amount of phosphorus may be attributed to the continuous application of phosphate fertilizers to crops which resulted in the buildup of phosphorus, as the efficiency of applied P is very low and it comes in the available form very slowly. The addition of organic manure with inorganic fertilizers had a beneficial effect in increasing phosphate availability (Dixit and Gupta, 2000). Plants take up only 10-40% of applied P during the growing season and the rest resides in the soil as less soluble products (Aulakh and Pasricha, 1999).

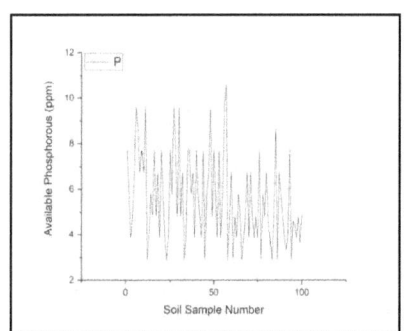 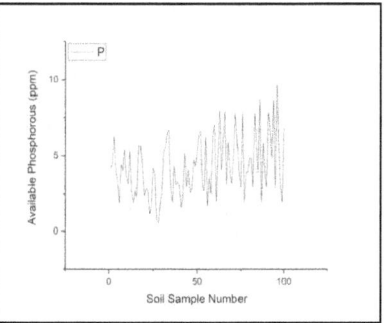

Graph-4.15: Mehsana District soil P   Graph-4.16: Narmada District soil P

Sample no	P	Sample no	P	Sample no	P	Sample no	P
1	7.704	26	5.778	51	5.778	76	7.704
2	5.778	27	9.630	52	3.852	77	2.889
3	3.852	28	7.704	53	7.704	78	5.778
4	4.815	29	4.815	54	3.852	79	4.815
5	6.741	30	9.630	55	5.778	80	6.741
6	9.630	31	4.815	56	9.630	81	4.815

Result and Discussion

7	8.667	32	6.741	57	10.593	82	3.852
8	6.741	33	2.889	58	2.889	83	2.889
9	7.704	34	3.852	59	4.815	84	4.815
10	6.741	35	7.704	60	6.741	85	8.667
11	9.630	36	7.704	61	2.889	86	2.889
12	2.889	37	5.778	62	4.815	87	6.741
13	3.852	38	6.741	63	3.852	88	5.778
14	5.778	39	3.852	64	5.778	89	4.815
15	4.815	40	7.704	65	4.815	90	3.852
16	7.704	41	5.778	66	2.889	91	3.326
17	4.815	42	4.815	67	3.852	92	3.852
18	6.741	43	3.852	68	4.815	93	7.704
19	3.852	44	7.704	69	6.741	94	2.889
20	7.704	45	2.889	70	3.852	95	4.597
21	5.778	46	5.778	71	6.741	96	4.476
22	3.852	47	6.741	72	4.815	97	3.852
23	2.889	48	9.630	73	3.852	98	4.815
24	3.852	49	4.815	74	4.815	99	3.638
25	7.704	50	7.704	75	3.852	100	4.872

Table-4.15: Soil Phosphorous Analysis of Mehsana District

Sample no	P	Sample no	P	Sample no	P	Sample no	P
1	4.168	26	3.781	51	6.352	76	7.798
2	4.420	27	0.773	52	6.587	77	1.949
3	6.234	28	0.571	53	3.075	78	3.899
4	4.083	29	1.798	54	2.706	79	3.899
5	3.260	30	2.504	55	6.167	80	4.874
6	1.899	31	5.243	56	1.697	81	4.874
7	4.420	32	5.545	57	3.579	82	2.924
8	4.016	33	6.436	58	2.504	83	7.798
9	5.411	34	6.688	59	6.369	84	5.848
10	3.647	35	2.907	60	7.041	85	3.899
11	3.109	36	1.949	61	1.995	86	8.773
12	5.277	37	4.302	62	4.938	87	1.949
13	2.689	38	3.092	63	7.963	88	5.848
14	1.899	39	3.260	64	4.059	89	3.899
15	2.672	40	2.974	65	5.959	90	2.924
16	2.336	41	1.546	66	7.909	91	7.798
17	5.680	42	2.437	67	3.106	92	6.823
18	5.680	43	5.209	68	5.946	93	4.874
19	4.117	44	2.941	69	3.899	94	8.773
20	2.369	45	4.067	70	3.119	95	2.924
21	2.840	46	2.605	71	4.874	96	9.747
22	2.756	47	2.874	72	7.798	97	5.848
23	1.143	48	4.722	73	5.848	98	2.924
24	1.664	49	4.302	74	3.899	99	1.949
25	4.201	50	5.125	75	2.924	100	6.823

Table-4.16: Soil Phosphorous Analysis of Narmada District

4.1.9. Potassium (ppm)

Data related to soil Potassium of the Mehsana District (Graph-4.17) and Narmada District (Graph-4.18) has been presented in Table-4.17 and Table-4.18 respectively. In the Mehsana District, the maximum soil K was 493.676ppm and the minimum was 55.060ppm; 264.901ppm soil K was the maximum and 18.452ppm was

Result and Discussion

the minimum for the Narmada District. Based on the limits suggested by Muhr *et al.*, (1963), the Mehsana District average K (121.276ppm) was high and the Narmada District average K (82.483ppm) was normal. Due to the continuous drain of K from the soil reserve over the years without its replenishment, the decrement in potassium content may start in both districts. And because of continuous cropping, the potassium status may not be sustained for a longer period (Pharande and Sonar, 1996).

Sample no	K	Sample no	K	Sample no	K	Sample no	K
1	55.060	26	100.074	51	114.955	76	84.821
2	114.955	27	110.119	52	180.060	77	72.173
3	90.030	28	55.060	53	204.985	78	88.170
4	155.134	29	139.881	54	103.051	79	61.384
5	204.985	30	110.119	55	202.381	80	58.408
6	129.836	31	155.134	56	82.961	81	132.440
7	139.881	32	129.836	57	239.955	82	104.539
8	165.179	33	219.866	58	102.679	83	97.098
9	100.074	34	84.821	59	70.685	84	100.446
10	84.821	35	149.926	60	79.985	85	104.539
11	110.119	36	55.060	61	68.452	86	127.604
12	155.134	37	110.119	62	78.125	87	81.845
13	174.851	38	139.881	63	78.869	88	107.143
14	204.985	39	114.955	64	493.676	89	98.586
15	55.060	40	84.821	65	126.488	90	104.539
16	129.836	41	155.134	66	140.997	91	119.048
17	204.985	42	129.836	67	96.354	92	84.821
18	114.955	43	84.821	68	130.580	93	110.491
19	170.015	44	110.119	69	187.128	94	155.134
20	204.985	45	155.134	70	117.932	95	92.262
21	125.000	46	129.836	71	141.369	96	100.818
22	84.821	47	174.851	72	84.821	97	145.833
23	75.149	48	90.030	73	145.833	98	92.262
24	65.104	49	55.060	74	90.402	99	98.958
25	90.030	50	100.074	75	98.958	100	93.006

Table-4.17: Soil Potassium Analysis of Mehsana District

Sample no	K	Sample no	K	Sample no	K	Sample no	K
1	18.452	26	92.262	51	36.905	76	234.913
2	46.131	27	73.810	52	73.810	77	189.929
3	18.452	28	46.131	53	55.357	78	209.922
4	36.905	29	101.488	54	83.036	79	109.959
5	46.131	30	156.845	55	46.131	80	139.948
6	73.810	31	92.262	56	36.905	81	29.989
7	27.679	32	64.583	57	27.679	82	49.981
8	83.036	33	46.131	58	73.810	83	34.987
9	18.452	34	73.810	59	64.583	84	34.987
10	73.810	35	64.583	60	36.905	85	29.989
11	92.262	36	83.036	61	154.942	86	39.985
12	83.036	37	18.452	62	209.922	87	44.983
13	64.583	38	64.583	63	189.929	88	34.987
14	46.131	39	46.131	64	264.901	89	59.978
15	73.810	40	27.679	65	204.924	90	49.981
16	129.167	41	46.131	66	254.905	91	79.970
17	55.357	42	27.679	67	199.926	92	34.987
18	55.357	43	64.583	68	214.920	93	29.989

19	46.131	44	73.810	69	114.957	94	44.983
20	36.905	45	83.036	70	189.929	95	29.989
21	46.131	46	18.452	71	209.922	96	54.980
22	55.357	47	64.583	72	189.929	97	34.987
23	73.810	48	55.357	73	139.948	98	49.981
24	119.940	49	49.814	74	164.939	99	64.976
25	27.679	50	46.131	75	224.916	100	34.987

Table-4.18: Soil Potassium Analysis of Narmada District

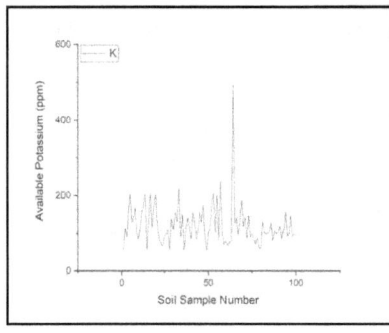 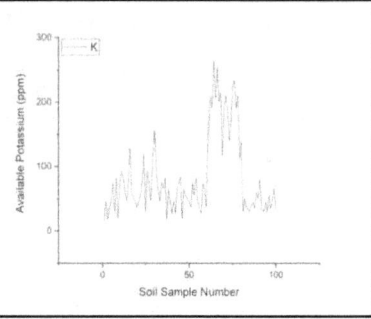

Graph-4.17: Mehsana District soil K   Graph-4.18: Narmada District soil K

4.1.10. Micronutrients

Micronutrients are essential elements that are used by plants in small quantities. Yields and quality of agricultural products increased with micronutrients application, therefore human and animal health is protected with feed of enrichment plant materials. Each essential element only when can perform its role in plant nutrition properly that other necessary elements are available in balanced ratios for plants in the soil. Here, Zink, Copper, Iron and Manganese were analyzed.

4.1.10.1. Zink (ppm)

Data related to soil micronutrient Zink of the Mehsana District (Graph-4.19) and Narmada District (Graph-4.20) has been presented in Table-4.19 and Table-4.20 respectively. In the Mehsana District, the maximum soil Zn was 2.080ppm and the minimum was 0.020ppm; and for the Narmada District, 3.950ppm soil Zn was the maximum and 0.590ppm was the minimum. Based on the criteria proposed by Takkar and Mann (1975), and Lindsay and Norvell (1978), the Mehsana District average Zn (0.539ppm) was low and the Narmada District average Zn (1.208ppm) was normal in range. Deficiency of Zn may be due to continuous extraction from the soil without addition or imbalance use of fertilizers.

Result and Discussion

Sample no	Zn	Sample no	Zn	Sample no	Zn	Sample no	Zn
1	0.800	26	0.820	51	0.960	76	0.020
2	0.400	27	0.520	52	0.900	77	0.140
3	0.320	28	0.580	53	0.300	78	0.280
4	0.300	29	0.660	54	0.360	79	0.220
5	0.600	30	0.300	55	0.940	80	0.480
6	0.240	31	0.220	56	1.140	81	0.660
7	0.440	32	0.260	57	2.080	82	0.300
8	0.360	33	0.360	58	0.660	83	0.260
9	0.700	34	0.580	59	0.560	84	0.280
10	0.580	35	0.440	60	0.160	85	0.560
11	0.380	36	0.640	61	0.200	86	0.400
12	0.760	37	0.500	62	0.260	87	0.160
13	0.320	38	0.340	63	0.160	88	0.480
14	0.460	39	0.700	64	1.260	89	0.620
15	0.560	40	0.540	65	0.720	90	0.320
16	0.500	41	0.240	66	0.780	91	0.360
17	0.260	42	0.360	67	0.460	92	0.560
18	0.680	43	0.560	68	0.820	93	0.290
19	0.560	44	0.280	69	1.020	94	1.120
20	0.520	45	1.120	70	0.760	95	1.010
21	0.740	46	0.880	71	0.180	96	0.910
22	0.520	47	1.160	72	0.220	97	0.640
23	0.400	48	0.700	73	0.640	98	0.360
24	0.420	49	0.720	74	0.360	99	0.230
25	0.600	50	0.840	75	0.220	100	0.380

Table-4.19: Soil Zink Analysis of Mehsana District

Sample no	Zn	Sample no	Zn	Sample no	Zn	Sample no	Zn
1	1.660	26	0.670	51	1.210	76	1.880
2	0.650	27	0.790	52	1.830	77	1.310
3	0.970	28	0.730	53	0.660	78	1.430
4	0.690	29	0.840	54	0.900	79	0.900
5	1.400	30	0.960	55	3.950	80	0.590
6	1.520	31	0.990	56	1.260	81	0.690
7	2.500	32	1.730	57	1.350	82	0.770
8	2.820	33	1.970	58	0.800	83	0.850
9	3.500	34	0.740	59	0.760	84	0.970
10	0.980	35	0.770	60	1.380	85	0.830
11	0.780	36	0.860	61	1.870	86	0.740
12	0.860	37	0.910	62	2.930	87	0.660
13	1.340	38	2.010	63	1.370	88	0.650
14	0.940	39	1.850	64	0.690	89	0.960
15	0.870	40	1.760	65	0.950	90	0.680
16	1.370	41	0.990	66	0.930	91	0.990
17	1.880	42	0.930	67	0.680	92	1.730
18	1.780	43	0.950	68	0.890	93	2.090
19	0.660	44	0.830	69	0.730	94	1.480
20	0.760	45	0.690	70	0.750	95	0.970
21	0.950	46	0.840	71	0.770	96	1.810
22	0.980	47	0.710	72	0.820	97	2.240
23	0.830	48	0.880	73	1.830	98	2.870
24	0.960	49	0.940	74	1.540	99	0.940
25	0.890	50	0.640	75	1.670	100	0.730

Table-4.20: Soil Zink Analysis of Narmada District

Result and Discussion

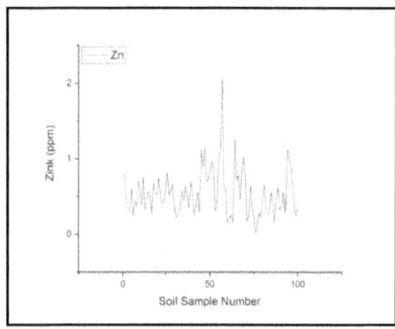

Graph-4.19: Mehsana District soil Zn

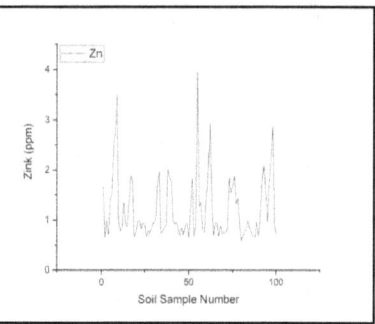

Graph-4.20: Narmada District soil Zn

4.1.10.2. Copper (ppm)

Data related to soil micronutrient Copper of the Mehsana District (Graph-4.21) and Narmada District (Graph-4.22) has been presented in Table-4.21 and Table-4.22 respectively. In the Mehsana District, the maximum soil Cu was 1.900ppm and the minimum was 0.260ppm; and for the Narmada District, 2.468ppm soil Cu was the maximum and 0.125ppm was the minimum. Based on the criteria proposed by Takkar and Mann (1975), and Lindsay and Norvell (1978), the Mehsana District average Cu (0.736ppm) was normal and the Narmada District average Cu (0.863ppm) was high in range.

Sample no	Cu	Sample no	Cu	Sample no	Cu	Sample no	Cu
1	0.360	26	1.100	51	0.680	76	0.980
2	0.420	27	0.280	52	0.360	77	1.020
3	0.380	28	0.360	53	0.380	78	1.120
4	0.520	29	0.960	54	0.940	79	0.660
5	0.560	30	0.440	55	1.900	80	0.740
6	1.000	31	0.560	56	0.600	81	0.860
7	0.520	32	0.500	57	0.820	82	1.180
8	1.020	33	0.720	58	0.560	83	0.800
9	0.520	34	1.000	59	0.700	84	1.000
10	0.660	35	0.260	60	0.800	85	1.460
11	0.420	36	0.640	61	0.720	86	1.060
12	0.420	37	0.560	62	0.640	87	1.180
13	0.260	38	0.640	63	0.700	88	1.180
14	0.820	39	0.460	64	1.020	89	0.820
15	0.400	40	0.700	65	0.760	90	0.960
16	1.160	41	0.420	66	0.680	91	0.970
17	0.300	42	0.820	67	0.860	92	0.900
18	0.340	43	0.900	68	0.920	93	0.310
19	0.440	44	0.300	69	0.920	94	1.200
20	0.560	45	1.200	70	0.980	95	1.020
21	0.660	46	0.280	71	1.300	96	0.870
22	0.700	47	0.260	72	0.680	97	0.880
23	0.740	48	0.560	73	0.880	98	0.990

Result and Discussion

24	0.400	49	0.420	74	0.980	99	0.820
25	0.440	50	0.700	75	0.820	100	1.000

Table-4.21: Soil Copper Analysis of Mehsana District

Sample no	Cu	Sample no	Cu	Sample no	Cu	Sample no	Cu
1	0.535	26	1.755	51	0.999	76	0.906
2	0.235	27	0.654	52	1.232	77	1.106
3	0.274	28	0.796	53	1.994	78	1.123
4	0.564	29	1.354	54	0.432	79	0.675
5	0.920	30	1.432	55	0.619	80	0.459
6	0.904	31	0.879	56	0.590	81	0.501
7	0.125	32	0.929	57	0.603	82	0.527
8	0.161	33	0.783	58	0.535	83	0.875
9	0.590	34	0.468	59	0.564	84	0.871
10	0.125	35	0.894	60	0.730	85	0.933
11	0.646	36	0.347	61	1.754	86	0.558
12	1.226	37	0.565	62	0.965	87	0.925
13	1.383	38	0.445	63	0.884	88	1.446
14	0.800	39	0.335	64	1.895	89	0.927
15	0.961	40	2.468	65	0.983	90	0.678
16	0.748	41	0.673	66	0.895	91	0.875
17	0.810	42	1.413	67	0.789	92	0.611
18	0.826	43	0.403	68	0.818	93	0.685
19	0.500	44	0.674	69	0.567	94	0.896
20	0.527	45	0.595	70	0.497	95	1.489
21	1.454	46	0.975	71	0.668	96	0.568
22	0.664	47	0.814	72	0.815	97	0.970
23	0.835	48	0.789	73	0.957	98	0.962
24	1.578	49	0.805	74	1.479	99	0.992
25	1.864	50	0.906	75	1.576	100	0.451

Table-4.22: Soil Copper Analysis of Narmada District

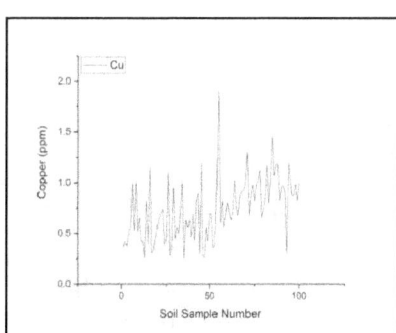

Graph-4.21: Mehsana District soil Cu   Graph-4.22: Narmada District soil Cu

4.1.10.3.   Iron (ppm)

Data related to soil micronutrient Iron of the Mehsana District (Graph-4.23) and Narmada District (Graph-4.24) has been presented in Table-4.23 and Table-4.24 respectively. In the Mehsana District, the maximum soil Fe was 13.360ppm and

Result and Discussion

the minimum was 3.800ppm; and 18.352ppm soil Fe was the maximum and 9.936ppm was the minimum for the Narmada District. Based on the criteria proposed by Takkar and Mann (1975), and Lindsay and Norvell (1978), the Mehsana District average Fe (7.765ppm) was recorded high and the Narmada District average Fe (13.862ppm) was recorded very high.

Sample no	Fe	Sample no	Fe	Sample no	Fe	Sample no	Fe
1	5.600	26	12.000	51	5.380	76	7.940
2	5.780	27	7.260	52	7.840	77	4.660
3	6.420	28	9.640	53	7.800	78	6.840
4	6.420	29	10.740	54	7.960	79	4.620
5	8.420	30	6.840	55	11.620	80	6.140
6	5.120	31	6.700	56	5.560	81	8.820
7	7.540	32	8.460	57	5.760	82	7.700
8	5.600	33	8.580	58	4.980	83	6.660
9	6.000	34	10.740	59	7.840	84	6.960
10	4.820	35	6.840	60	8.940	85	9.840
11	4.980	36	5.560	61	7.020	86	9.040
12	7.520	37	5.600	62	7.660	87	6.960
13	5.460	38	7.540	63	7.460	88	7.380
14	5.900	39	10.760	64	6.240	89	7.540
15	7.200	40	7.420	65	6.400	90	8.580
16	13.360	41	11.600	66	5.300	91	8.650
17	9.620	42	7.800	67	3.800	92	11.740
18	12.300	43	11.740	68	5.000	93	8.990
19	8.420	44	8.960	69	5.940	94	7.520
20	6.220	45	7.520	70	7.940	95	8.340
21	8.000	46	10.840	71	10.940	96	8.980
22	7.560	47	8.520	72	6.080	97	9.920
23	8.520	48	11.380	73	9.920	98	9.050
24	6.440	49	7.640	74	9.040	99	8.720
25	4.360	50	6.560	75	8.720	100	8.990

Table-4.23: Soil Iron Analysis of Mehsana District

Sample no	Fe	Sample no	Fe	Sample no	Fe	Sample no	Fe
1	10.000	26	14.670	51	13.740	76	12.482
2	12.220	27	13.280	52	12.000	77	16.320
3	14.540	28	14.573	53	15.380	78	13.850
4	15.260	29	13.580	54	12.940	79	11.390
5	15.100	30	17.480	55	13.900	80	14.390
6	15.700	31	11.942	56	11.500	81	11.500
7	17.710	32	12.430	57	12.400	82	16.240
8	16.800	33	15.380	58	10.000	83	13.430
9	12.300	34	18.352	59	11.600	84	12.340
10	11.730	35	18.340	60	13.500	85	11.330
11	10.930	36	13.530	61	12.490	86	16.111
12	9.936	37	11.370	62	13.580	87	12.474
13	17.234	38	15.780	63	13.230	88	15.380
14	16.380	39	12.583	64	17.160	89	13.820
15	14.964	40	14.820	65	16.980	90	12.320
16	14.300	41	11.980	66	10.450	91	13.720
17	16.500	42	17.130	67	10.990	92	11.360
18	17.100	43	16.363	68	11.980	93	15.730
19	10.500	44	12.482	69	12.110	94	13.363
20	16.400	45	13.280	70	12.830	95	11.712

21	12.330	46	11.001	71	11.530	96	12.600
22	14.540	47	10.830	72	13.480	97	17.500
23	16.220	48	18.000	73	12.440	98	16.100
24	18.009	49	12.842	74	15.280	99	13.730
25	11.450	50	14.473	75	15.950	100	14.940

Table-4.24: Soil Iron Analysis of Narmada District

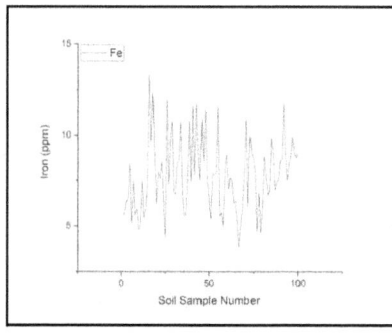 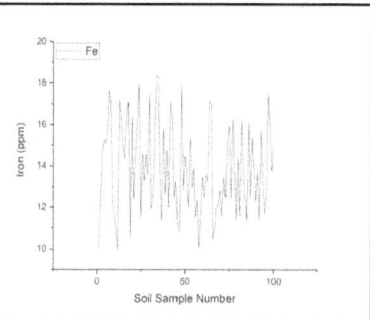

Graph-4.23: Mehsana District soil Fe   Graph-4.24: Narmada District soil Fe

4.1.10.4.   Manganese (ppm)

Data related to soil micronutrient Manganese of the Mehsana District (Graph-4.25) and Narmada District (Graph-4.26) has been presented in Table-4.25 and Table-4.26 respectively. In the Mehsana District, the maximum soil Mn was 16.060ppm and the minimum was 5.320ppm; and for the Narmada District, 78.943ppm soil Mn was the maximum and 1.123ppm was the minimum. Based on the criteria proposed by Takkar and Mann (1975), and Lindsay and Norvell (1978), the Mehsana District average Mn (10.516ppm) and the Narmada District average Mn (23.347ppm) both were recorded very high.

Sample no	Mn	Sample no	Mn	Sample no	Mn	Sample no	Mn
1	13.300	26	15.780	51	15.220	76	9.380
2	12.440	27	9.360	52	14.500	77	11.620
3	8.940	28	10.780	53	9.100	78	10.720
4	9.800	29	11.260	54	14.060	79	9.920
5	9.200	30	11.160	55	10.560	80	14.240
6	6.600	31	6.400	56	10.380	81	11.380
7	10.660	32	11.760	57	10.740	82	9.800
8	8.380	33	10.660	58	12.260	83	11.640
9	8.780	34	13.040	59	14.440	84	9.960
10	7.120	35	7.620	60	13.180	85	11.200
11	6.920	36	12.160	61	7.800	86	12.220
12	7.240	37	16.060	62	6.940	87	10.640
13	11.000	38	11.400	63	6.880	88	13.400
14	7.840	39	10.760	64	14.660	89	10.960
15	8.720	40	8.420	65	9.320	90	8.640
16	10.800	41	7.500	66	10.020	91	9.500

Result and Discussion

17	8.640	42	11.520	67	9.720	92	7.410
18	10.540	43	7.420	68	10.600	93	15.210
19	6.580	44	15.100	69	12.960	94	10.440
20	6.740	45	10.440	70	7.520	95	12.140
21	5.320	46	11.400	71	10.600	96	11.110
22	11.040	47	9.160	72	8.860	97	13.090
23	9.420	48	7.100	73	13.060	98	14.500
24	7.640	49	12.220	74	14.500	99	8.240
25	10.720	50	10.000	75	8.480	100	15.010

Table-4.25: Soil Manganese Analysis of Mehsana District

Sample no	Mn	Sample no	Mn	Sample no	Mn	Sample no	Mn
1	51.500	26	78.943	51	9.340	76	14.843
2	12.345	27	12.343	52	7.310	77	34.321
3	45.643	28	13.334	53	9.999	78	16.544
4	63.453	29	11.232	54	8.743	79	27.655
5	23.443	30	15.430	55	24.332	80	9.854
6	7.540	31	12.532	56	14.800	81	14.550
7	17.050	32	18.432	57	19.050	82	14.930
8	56.820	33	13.443	58	11.590	83	32.443
9	15.080	34	9.143	59	14.630	84	43.542
10	12.453	35	25.432	60	16.200	85	64.543
11	53.400	36	43.221	61	18.334	86	75.634
12	17.320	37	13.432	62	18.343	87	7.453
13	45.430	38	14.221	63	24.330	88	34.565
14	11.332	39	13.543	64	12.132	89	17.143
15	13.332	40	22.121	65	15.632	90	23.453
16	16.070	41	19.220	66	17.643	91	34.524
17	47.450	42	1.211	67	18.743	92	13.423
18	37.810	43	1.123	68	17.684	93	15.640
19	54.550	44	9.421	69	15.332	94	15.420
20	75.030	45	7.532	70	42.342	95	33.523
21	12.364	46	9.850	71	34.432	96	16.210
22	44.534	47	8.442	72	12.343	97	29.200
23	65.445	48	9.340	73	16.544	98	28.680
24	9.665	49	14.532	74	12.332	99	28.949
25	9.734	50	8.840	75	15.848	100	34.584

Table-4.26: Soil Manganese Analysis of Narmada District

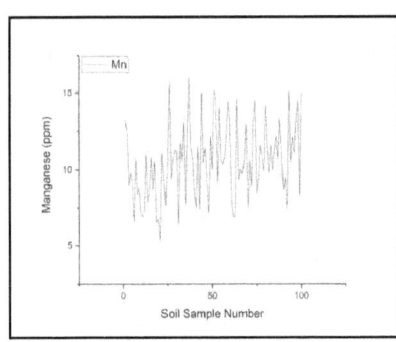 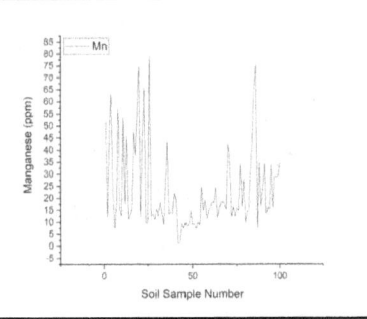

Graph-4.25: Mehsana District soil Mn   Graph-4.26: Narmada District soil Mn

Result and Discussion

4.1.11. Colony Forming Units (cfus/ml)

Data related to soil microbial Colony Forming Units of the Mehsana District (Graph-4.27) and Narmada District (Graph-4.28) has been presented in Table-4.27 and Table-4.28 respectively. In the Mehsana District, the maximum soil CFUs was 7910550cfus/ml and the minimum was 35040cfus/ml; and for the Narmada District, 8920100cfus/ml soil CFUs was the maximum and 23380cfus/ml was the minimum. Colony forming units were recorded very high in the Narmada District compare to the Mehsana District that indicates the presence of good soil Microbial activity in the District agriculture soil.

Sample no	CFUs	Sample no	CFUs	Sample no	CFUs	Sample no	CFUs
1	978950	26	1972030	51	279670	76	995410
2	2046750	27	452300	52	3102020	77	823420
3	2159080	28	764550	53	664460	78	754320
4	1923020	29	263140	54	964730	79	342310
5	2610650	30	752330	55	1256510	80	274680
6	2409650	31	3042670	56	895410	81	971512
7	298560	32	2762020	57	723420	82	7910550
8	189230	33	464460	58	654320	83	5610040
9	696520	34	564730	59	942310	84	7210200
10	1582330	35	1750010	60	774680	85	1697020
11	998510	36	945410	61	3728500	86	3720450
12	982210	37	723420	62	3157460	87	832800
13	896240	38	654320	63	985240	88	879200
14	796220	39	342310	64	856120	89	791000
15	924660	40	274680	65	363410	90	910000
16	242770	41	4728500	66	2002030	91	942010
17	184560	42	2357460	67	99300	92	2865750
18	195320	43	995240	68	89230	93	3016420
19	202850	44	756120	69	65040	94	851230
20	176620	45	463410	70	38400	95	2746120
21	2728500	46	1202030	71	299670	96	4251220
22	2157460	47	99390	72	3162020	97	698910
23	985240	48	79230	73	664460	98	726720
24	756120	49	35040	74	564730	99	951210
25	263410	50	98400	75	1756510	100	661020

Table-4.27: Soil Colony Forming Units Analysis of Mehsana District

Sample no	CFUs	Sample no	CFUs	Sample no	CFUs	Sample no	CFUs
1	94210	26	251220	51	1728500	76	941320
2	2865750	27	908910	52	5574060	77	56400
3	3016420	28	626720	53	2852040	78	48900
4	451230	29	851210	54	3561020	79	97210
5	2746120	30	501020	55	2634010	80	23380
6	4251220	31	960240	56	4720030	81	8920100
7	398910	32	850600	57	542300	82	2865750
8	426720	33	2012600	58	294550	83	3016420
9	451210	34	980550	59	663140	84	4512320
10	651020	35	645070	60	502330	85	2746120
11	2561000	36	941300	61	798230	86	4251220

Result and Discussion

12	734970	37	264000	62	984200	87	2398910
13	921380	38	34800	63	654780	88	426720
14	1276100	39	231010	64	947240	89	451210
15	794210	40	123080	65	891630	90	601000
16	812310	41	5623230	66	984130	91	6248060
17	342400	42	6459600	67	456230	92	7512320
18	456470	43	5461200	68	327700	93	8412500
19	798160	44	4506700	69	582310	94	6456040
20	654970	45	3201400	70	328400	95	7942530
21	294210	46	2379420	71	846240	96	984510
22	865750	47	465120	72	645600	97	498010
23	2316420	48	405060	73	2612660	98	694040
24	651230	49	762100	74	984550	99	945060
25	3746120	50	574500	75	645970	100	564070

Table-4.28: Soil Colony Forming Units Analysis of Narmada District

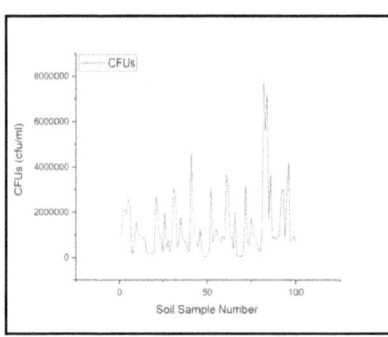 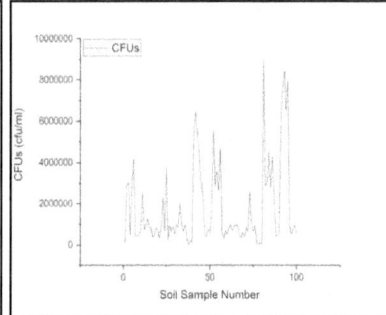

Graph-4.27: Mehsana District soil CFUs   Graph-4.28: Narmada District soil CFUs

4.2.   Statistical Analyses: Soil Analyzed Data

4.2.1.   Mehsana District

Three statistical tests were performed for the district. 1. Descriptive Statistics of the Mehsana district and showed the central tendency and measures of dispersion. 2. One-Sample T-Test was done to get the significant mean comparison values. 3. Bivariate Correlations, possible relations between the analyzed soil parameters were done.

4.2.1.1.   Descriptive Statistics

Table-4.29 shows the Descriptive Statistics for the Mehsana District. The test was performed for the 100 samples of the Mehsana district. Soil physical parameters are Moisture, pH, Electrical conductivity, and Bulk Density. The Moisture mean was 14 % with a Standard Deviation of 7.97. It was spreading in the range of

Result and Discussion

46.95 percent. Maximum pH noted was 8.5 and minimum was 7.24 while average pH was 7.84 ± 0.031S.E. The variance was 0.096. The mean Electrical conductivity was 0.347 mmhos/cm with a deviation of 0.23 in the district. The average Bulk Density was 1.372 gm/cm^3 and all the results were between 1.22 to 1.59 gm/cm^3.

Soil Parameter	N	Range	Minimum	Maximum	Mean	±Std. Error	±Std. Deviation
Moisture	100	46.95	4.31	51.26	14.0786	0.79723	7.97234
pH	100	1.26	7.24	8.5	7.8474	0.03103	0.31034
EC	100	2.05	0.15	2.2	0.3476	0.02298	0.2298
BD	100	0.37	1.22	1.59	1.372	0.00877	0.08768
OC	100	0.93	0.02	0.95	0.4074	0.02009	0.20091
N	100	0.08	0	0.08	0.0351	0.00173	0.01732
P	100	7.7	2.89	10.59	5.5636	0.19614	1.96144
K	100	438.62	55.06	493.68	121.276	5.59462	55.94625
Fe	100	9.56	3.8	13.36	7.7654	0.20162	2.01618
Zn	100	2.06	0.02	2.08	0.539	0.03086	0.30856
Cu	100	1.64	0.26	1.9	0.7364	0.03033	0.30327
Mn	100	10.74	5.32	16.06	10.5159	0.24804	2.48044
CFUs	100	7875510	35040	7910550	1334518	143488.91	1434889.1
N=100 Soil sample							

Table-4.29: Descriptive Statistics for the Mehsana District

Organic carbon, macronutrients, and micronutrients are soil chemical parameters. Organic carbon and Nitrogen were estimated in percentage while other parameters were in ppm. The mean OC and Nitrogen were 0.41 and 0.035 %. OC Std. deviation was 0.201. Maximum OC was 0.95 and minimum was 0.02 %. Here, the Nitrogen minimum value is not zero but it was <0.002 %. The average Phosphorus and Potassium were 5.56 and 126.28 ppm respectively. The minimum P and K values were 2.89 and 55.06 while the maximum P and K values were 10.59 and 493.68 ppm accordingly. The averages for Micronutrients were 7.76 for Fe, 0.539 for Zn, 0.736 for Cu, and 10.516 for Mn. The Std. Deviation was <2.0 for Fe and Mn while 0.30 for the Zn and Cu. CFUs, the soil microbial parameter was showing an average colony of 1334518. The maximum count was 7910550 while the minimum count was 35040.

4.2.1.2. One-Sample T-Test

Soil Parameter	T	Df	Significance (2-tailed)	Mean Difference	95% Confidence Interval of the Difference	
					Lower	Upper
Moisture	17.659	99	0.000	14.0786	12.4967	15.6605
pH	252.868	99	0.000	7.8474	7.7858	7.909
EC	15.126	99	0.000	0.3476	0.302	0.3932
BD	156.477	99	0.000	1.37203	1.3546	1.3894
OC	20.278	99	0.000	0.4074	0.3675	0.4473
N	20.278	99	0.000	0.03512	0.0317	0.0386
P	28.365	99	0.000	5.56357	5.1744	5.9528
K	21.677	99	0.000	121.27604	110.1751	132.377
Fe	38.515	99	0.000	7.7654	7.3653	8.1655
Zn	17.468	99	0.000	0.539	0.4778	0.6002
Cu	24.282	99	0.000	0.7364	0.6762	0.7966
Mn	42.395	99	0.000	10.5159	10.0237	11.0081
CFUs	9.3	99	0.000	1334518	1049804.9	1619231.2

N=100 Soil sample

Table-4.30: One-Sample Test for the Mehsana District

SPSS Statistics generates two main tables of output for the One-Sample T-Test. One table is One Sample Statistics and the other is the One-Sample Test. One-Sample Statistics provides basic information about the selected variables (soil parameters), including the valid (nonmissing) sample size (n), mean, standard deviation, and standard error which is discussed in Descriptive Statistics (Table-4.29). The One-Sample Test table reported the result of the One-Sample T-Test. The test statistic, t statistic value is calculated by dividing the mean difference (E) by the standard error mean (from the One-Sample Statistics table). The degrees of freedom for the test, for a One-Sample T-Test, df = n - 1 (where n=number of the sample). The Significance (2-tailed) or p-value is corresponding to the test statistic. The difference between the "observed" sample mean (from the One-Sample Statistics) and the "expected" mean (the specified test value) is the Mean Difference. The confidence interval for the difference between the specified test value and the sample mean. Based on Significance (2-tailed) or $p < 0.001$, we can conclude that the mean of the sample is significantly different than the average of the overall.

Result and Discussion

The mean was compared with the One-Sample T-Test. Table-4.30 shows the One-Sample Test for the Mehsana District. There were 100 samples of the Mehsana district. Therefore, the degree of freedom is 99 for a sample. 95% Confidence Interval of the Difference in lower and upper limits was near to the mean difference values. Test values were also noticeable for all the parameters. Significant (2-tailed or p-value) were less than <0.005 for all the soil parameters that indicated that mean of the all parameters was significantly different for the district soil samples.

4.2.1.3. Bivariate Correlations

This test was performed in SPSS Statistics subscription software to find inter-correlations of soil parameters. In the Correlations output table, there were rows and columns for each tested variable and that contain numbers that represent variable crossings. In the rows and columns crossing over of variables, there were two same values for Pearson's r (Pearson Correlation), Significance (2-tailed) values and Number of samples (N).

4.2.1.3.1. Pearson's r-value

Pearson's r-value shows as Pearson Correlation were two variable crosses. Pearson's r-value close to 1 indicates a strong relationship between two variables. It means changes in one variable are strongly correlated with the second variable. Pearson's r-value close to 0 indicates a weak relationship between two variables. This means that changes in one variable are not correlated with changes in the second variable. Now, Positive Pearson's r value indicates that as one variable increases in value, the second variable also increases in value. Similarly, a decrease in one variable value than a second variable value also decreases. This is called a positive correlation. While negative Pearson's r-value indicates a negative correlation. This means that as one variable increases in value, the second variable decreases in value.

4.2.1.3.2. Significance (2-Tailed) value

Significance (2-Tailed) values suggest if there is a statistically significant correlation between two variables. If the Significance (2-Tailed) value is greater than 0.05 which means, there is no statistically significant correlation between the two

Result and Discussion

variables. This means increases or decreases in one variable do not significantly relate to increases or decreases in the second variable. And if the Significance (2-Tailed) value is less than or equal to 0.05 which means, there is a statistically significant correlation between the two variables. This means increases or decreases in one variable do significantly relate to increases or decreases in your second variable.

Table-4.31 shows the possible Correlations for the Mehsana District agricultural soil. Moisture content showed a negatively strong correlation with Bulk Density, Pearson r value was -0.292 and Significance (2-tailed) was 0.003 which indicated a significant correlation. That means as the moisture content increases, BD is decreasing and vice versa. And strong positive correlation between Moisture and copper was found with 0.300 Pearson's r-value and 0.002 significance (2-tailed), a significant correlation. That shows that Moisture and Cu both increasing with each other or decreasing. While a negative correlation between Moisture and Phosphorus was also noted. pH value showed a strong negative correlation with Organic Carbon, Nitrogen, Copper, and Manganese. Pearson's r-value was -0.361 for OC and N; -0.271 was for Cu and Mn. These correlations were significant with Significance (2-tailed) of 0.0 for OC and N; 0.006 for Cu and Mn. These correlations of pH were suggested that as the pH increases, OC, N, Cu, and Mn decrease and vice versa. A significant positive correlation was recorded between Electrical Conductivity and Zink, Pearson's r-value was 0.249 and Significance (2-tailed) was 0.013; EC and Zn increase or decreases together. Bulk Density was strongly negatively correlated with OC and N while positively correlated with Iron. A strong positive correlation was noted between OC and N with 1.00 Pearson's r-value. P showed a significant negative correlation with Cu and Colony Forming Units. The positive correlation of Zn was found with Potassium and negative with CFUs. There was also a positive correlation between Fe and Cu.

Result and Discussion

Soil Parameter		Moisture	pH	FC	BD	OC	N	P	K	Fe	Zn	Cu	Mn	CFUs
Moisture	Pearson Correlation	1	-0.171	-0.069	-.292**	0.171	0.171	-.251*	0.071	-0.076	-0.15	.330**	0.09	0.107
	Sig (2-tailed)		0.089	0.494	0.003	0.089	0.089	0.012	0.48	0.454	0.137	0.002	0.373	0.289
pH	Pearson Correlation	-0.171	1	0.035	0.025	-.361**	-.361**	0.104	-0.013	0.021	-0.025	-.271**	-.271**	-0.069
	Sig (2-tailed)	0.089		0.726	0.803	0	0	0.303	0.901	0.838	0.803	0.006	0.006	0.494
FC	Pearson Correlation	-0.069	0.035	1	0.135	0.123	0.123	-0.111	0.156	0.012	.249*	0.006	0.099	0.094
	Sig (2-tailed)	0.494	0.726		0.181	0.223	0.223	0.276	0.12	0.905	0.013	0.56	0.329	0.353
BD	Pearson Correlation	-.292**	0.025	0.135	1	0.181	0.181	-0.075	-0.14	.215*	0.086	-0.038	0.011	-0.067
	Sig (2-tailed)	0.003	0.803	0.181		0.003	0.003	0.45	0.26	0.032	0.396	0.708	0.915	0.527
OC	Pearson Correlation	0.171	-.361**	0.123	0.181	1	1.000**	0.028	0.091	0.113	0.17	0.191	-0.017	.646
	Sig (2-tailed)	0.089	0	0.223	0.003		0	0.778	0.368	0.255	0.091	0.057	0.865	.651
N	Pearson Correlation	0.171	-.361**	0.123	-.293**	1.000**	1	0.028	0.091	0.113	0.17	0.191	-0.017	.646
	Sig (2-tailed)	0.089	0	0.223	0.003	0		0.778	0.368	0.255	0.091	0.057	0.865	.651
P	Pearson Correlation	-.251*	0.104	-0.11	-0.076	0.028	0.028	1	0.054	-0.083	0.145	-.198*	-0.024	-.218*
	Sig (2-tailed)	0.012	0.303	0.276	0.45	0.778	0.778		0.591	0.429	0.151	0.048	0.816	0.029
K	Pearson Correlation	0.071	-0.013	0.156	-0.114	0.091	0.091	0.054	1	0.037	.366**	0.06	0.008	-0.074
	Sig (2-tailed)	0.48	0.901	0.12	0.26	0.368	0.368	0.591		0.715	0	0.555	0.939	0.463
Fe	Pearson Correlation	-0.076	0.021	0.012	-.215*	0.113	0.113	-0.083	0.007	1	-0.015	.209*	0.071	0.041
	Sig (2-tailed)	0.454	0.838	0.905	0.032	0.255	0.255	0.409	0.943		0.885	0.037	0.482	.687
Zn	Pearson Correlation	-0.15	-0.025	.249*	0.086	0.17	0.17	0.145	-0.06	-0.015	1	0.055	0.165	-.218*
	Sig (2-tailed)	0.137	0.803	0.013	0.396	0.091	0.091	0.15	0.555	0.885		0.584	0.101	0.029
Cu	Pearson Correlation	.300**	-.271**	-0.059	-0.038	0.191	0.191	-.198*	0.006	.209*	0.584	1	0.147	.682
	Sig (2-tailed)	0.002	0.006	0.56	0.708	0.057	0.057	0.048	0.955	0.037	0.055		0.144	.415
Mn	Pearson Correlation	0.09	-.271**	0.099	0.011	-0.017	-0.017	-0.024	0.008	0.071	0.165	0.147	1	-0.097
	Sig (2-tailed)	0.373	0.006	0.329	0.915	0.865	0.865	0.816	0.939	0.482	0.101	0.144		0.338
CFUs	Pearson Correlation	0.107	-0.069	0.094	-0.064	0.046	0.046	-.218*	-0.074	0.041	-.218*	0.082	-0.097	1
	Sig (2-tailed)	0.289	0.494	0.353	0.527	0.651	0.651	0.029	0.463	0.687	0.029	0.415	0.338	

**. Correlation is significant at the 0.01 level (2-tailed).
*. Correlation is significant at the 0.05 level (2-tailed).
N=100 Soil sample

Table-4.31: Correlation table for Mehsana District

Result and Discussion

4.2.2. Narmada District

Three statistical tests were performed for the district. 1. Descriptive Statistics of the district soil analyzed data that showed the central tendency and measures of dispersion. 2. One-Sample T-Test was done to get the significant mean comparison values. 3. Bivariate Correlations to find possible relations between the soil parameters were done.

4.2.2.1. Descriptive Statistics

Table-4.32 shows the Descriptive Statistics for the Narmada District. The test was performed for the 100 samples. Soil physical parameters are Moisture, pH, Electrical conductivity, and Bulk Density. The Moisture mean was 28.32 % with a Standard Deviation of 6.68. It was spreading in the range of 37.37 %. Maximum pH noted was 7.43 and minimum was 5.93 while average pH was 6.68 ± 0.041 S.E. The mean Electrical conductivity was recorded at 0.39 mmhos/cm and the deviation was 0.05. The 0.43 mmhos/cm value was noted as the maximum EC and 0.04 as the minimum value. The Average Bulk Density was 1.41gm/cm^3 and all the bulk density results were between 1.09 to 1.073 gm/cm^3.

Soil Parameter	N	Range	Minimum	Maximum	Mean	±Std. Error	±Std. Deviation
Moisture	100	37.37	14.19	51.56	28.3194	0.66767	6.67668
pH	100	1.5	5.93	7.43	6.667	0.04118	0.41184
EC	100	0.39	0.04	0.43	0.0939	0.00544	0.05444
BD	100	0.65	1.09	1.73	1.4142	0.01476	0.14765
OC	100	4.08	0.11	4.19	1.608	0.10989	1.09888
N	100	0.35	0.01	0.36	0.1386	0.00947	0.09472
P	100	9.18	0.57	9.75	4.2759	0.19792	1.97917
K	100	246.45	18.45	264.9	82.4825	6.19551	61.95514
Fe	100	8.42	9.94	18.35	13.8622	0.22019	2.20191
Zn	100	3.36	0.59	3.95	1.208	0.06447	0.64466
Cu	100	2.34	0.12	2.47	0.8625	0.0424	0.42396
Mn	100	77.82	1.12	78.94	23.3474	1.72708	17.27077
CFUs	100	8896720	23380	8920100	1799751.4	207995.8	2079958

N=100 Soil sample

Table-4.32: Descriptive Statistics for the Narmada District

Result and Discussion

Organic carbon, macronutrients, and micronutrients are soil chemical parameters. Organic carbon and Nitrogen were estimated in percentage while other parameters were in ppm. The mean OC and Nitrogen were 1.61 % and 0.14 % accordingly. Standard Deviation was 1.1 for OC and 0.1 for N. 4.19 % was noted as the maximum OC in the district soil samples, while 0.36 % maximum N. The average of Phosphorus and Potassium were 4.28 and 82.48 ppm respectively. The minimum P and K values were 0.57 and 18.45 while the maximum P and K values were 9.75 and 264.9 ppm accordingly. The averages for micronutrients were 13.86 for Fe, 1.21 for Zn, 0.86 for Cu, and 23.35 for Mn. CFUs, the soil microbial parameter was showing an average colony of 1799751. The maximum count was 8920100 while the minimum count was 23380.

4.2.2.2. One-Sample T-Test

Soil Parameter	Test Value = 0					
	T	Df	Sig. (2-tailed)	Mean Difference	95% Confidence Interval of the Difference	
					Lower	Upper
Moisture	42.415	99	0.000	28.3194	26.9946	29.6442
pH	161.882	99	0.000	6.667	6.5853	6.7487
EC	17.249	99	0.000	0.0939	0.0831	0.1047
BD	95.778	99	0.000	1.41415	1.3849	1.4434
OC	14.633	99	0.000	1.608	1.39	1.826
N	14.633	99	0.000	0.13861	0.1198	0.1574
P	21.605	99	0.000	4.27593	3.8832	4.6686
K	13.313	99	0.000	82.4825	70.1893	94.7757
Fe	62.955	99	0.000	13.86216	13.4253	14.2991
Zn	18.738	99	0.000	1.208	1.0801	1.3359
Cu	20.345	99	0.000	0.86253	0.7784	0.9467
Mn	13.518	99	0.000	23.34743	19.9205	26.7743
CFUs	8.653	99	0.000	1799751	1387043	2212460
N=100 Soil sample						

Table-4.33: One-Sample Test for the Narmada District

SPSS Statistics generates two main tables of output for the One-Sample T-test. One table is One Sample Statistics and the other is One-Sample Test. One-Sample Statistics provides basic information about the selected variables (soil parameters), including the valid (nonmissing) sample size (n), mean, standard

Result and Discussion

deviation, and standard error which is discussed in Descriptive Statistics (Table-4.32). The One-Sample Test table reports the result of the One-Sample T-Test. And more about the One-Sample T-Test is described in (4.2.1.2 One-Sample T-Test).

The mean was compared with the One-Sample T-Test. Table-4.33 shows the One-Sample Test for the Narmada District. There were 100 samples of the district. Therefore, the degree of freedom is 99 for a sample. 95% Confidence Interval of the Difference in lower and upper limits was near to the mean difference values. Test values were also noticeable for all the parameters. Significant (2-tailed or p-value) were less than <0.005 for all the soil parameters that indicated that mean of the all parameters was significantly different for the district soil samples.

4.2.2.3. Bivariate Correlations

This test was performed to find inter-correlations. Pearson's r (Pearson Correlation), Significance (2-tailed) values are important to find or build correlations between variables or parameters. And more about Bivariate Correlations is described in (4.2.1.3 Bivariate Correlations).

Table-4.34 shows the possible Correlations for the Narmada district agricultural soil. Moisture content showed a significant strong positive correlation with pH and K, Pearson's r-value was 0.359 for pH and 0.367 for K. That means as the moisture content increases or decreases, pH and K values follow. And the significant strong negative correlation of Moisture was noted in OC and N where Pearson's r was -0.390 and Significance (2-tailed) was 0.00. That shows that as the Moisture increases, OC and N decrease or vice versa. pH value showed a strong negative correlation with EC, Organic Carbon, and Nitrogen; Positively correlated with BD and K. All pH correlations were significant based on Significance (2-tailed) values. Electrical Conductivity was significantly correlated with BD, OC, N, and K where BD and K were negatively correlated while OC and N were noted positively correlated. Significantly correlations were also recorded for BD with OC, N, P, Fe, and CFUs. In which, OC, N, and Fe were negatively correlated while P and CFUs showed positive correlations. OC also showed a positive correlation with N and Zn but a strong negative correlation for K. K was showing a negative correlation with N

Result and Discussion

and CFUs while positive for Copper. There was a positive correlation between N and Zn. Person's r-value was 0.202.

Soil Parameter		Moisture	pH	EC	BD	OC	N	P	K	Fe	Zn	Cu	Mn	CFUs
Moisture	Pearson Correlation	1	.359**	-0.002	0.166	-.393**	-.390**	0.034	.357**	0.372	-0.114	0.142	0.45	-0.05
	Sig. (2-tailed)		0	0.985	0.099	0	0	0.741	0	0.479	0.258	0.155	0.15	0.375
pH	Pearson Correlation	.359**	1	-.272**	.289**	-.623**	-.623**	0.126	.256**	0.057	-0.028	0.043	-0.033	0.14
	Sig. (2-tailed)	0		0.006	0	0	0	0.122	0.007	0.506	0.784	0.665	0.748	0.164
EC	Pearson Correlation	-0.002	-.272**	1	-.257**	.460**	.400**	-0.031	-.210*	0.344	0.055	-0.123	-0.014	-0.05
	Sig. (2-tailed)	0.985	0.006		0.007	0	0	0.758	0.036	0.556	0.59	0.223	0.888	0.372
BD	Pearson Correlation	0.166	.289**	-.257**	1	-.323**	-.323**	.307**	0.11	-.212*	-0.001	-0.066	0.057	.221*
	Sig. (2-tailed)	0.099	0	0.007		0.001	0.001	0.002	0.274	0.035	0.993	0.516	0.57	0.027
OC	Pearson Correlation	-.393**	-.623**	.460**	-.323**	1	1.000**	0.16	-.333**	0.036	-.202*	-0.15	-.374**	-0.15
	Sig. (2-tailed)	0	0	0	0.001		0	0.112	0.001	0.726	0.043	0.136	0	0.136
N	Pearson Correlation	-.390**	-.623**	.460**	-.323**	1.000**	1	0.16	-.333**	0.036	-.202*	-0.15	-.463**	-0.15
	Sig. (2-tailed)	0	0	0	0.001	0		0.112	0.001	0.726	0.043	0.136	0	0.136
P	Pearson Correlation	0.034	0.126	-0.031	.307**	0.16	0.16	1	0.073	-0.086	0.195	-0.162	0.024	0.13
	Sig. (2-tailed)	0.741	0.122	0.758	0.002	0.112	0.112		0.473	0.396	0.051	0.106	0.809	0.196
K	Pearson Correlation	.357**	.256**	-.210*	0.11	-.333**	-.333**	0.073	1	0.332	-0.035	.213*	-0.125	-.305**
	Sig. (2-tailed)	0	0.007	0.036	0.274	0.001	0.001	0.473		0.729	0.729	0.033	0.216	0.002
Fe	Pearson Correlation	0.372	0.057	0.344	-.212*	0.036	0.036	-0.086	0.332	1	0.145	0.157	0.09	-0.15
	Sig. (2-tailed)	0.479	0.506	0.556	0.035	0.726	0.726	0.396	0.984		0.151	0.118	0.374	0.255
Zn	Pearson Correlation	-0.114	-0.028	0.055	-0.001	-.202*	-.202*	0.195	-0.035	0.145	1	0.118	0.374	-0.027
	Sig. (2-tailed)	0.258	0.784	0.993	0.993	0.043	0.043	0.051	0.729	0.151		-0.045	-0.042	0.789
Cu	Pearson Correlation	0.142	0.043	-0.123	-0.066	-0.15	-0.15	-0.162	.213*	0.157	-0.045	1	-0.103	-0.019
	Sig. (2-tailed)	0.155	0.665	0.223	0.516	0.136	0.136	0.106	0.033	0.118	0.653		0.309	0.852
Mn	Pearson Correlation	0.45	-0.033	-0.014	0.057	-.374**	-.374**	0.024	-0.125	0.09	-0.042	-0.103	1	-0.105
	Sig. (2-tailed)	0.15	0.748	0.888	0.57	0	0	0.809	0.216	0.374	0.58	0.309		0.299
CFUs	Pearson Correlation	-0.05	0.14	-0.05	.221*	-0.15	-0.15	0.13	-.305**	-0.15	-0.027	-0.019	-0.105	1
	Sig. (2-tailed)	0.375	0.164	0.372	0.027	0.136	0.136	0.196	0.002	0.255	0.789	0.852	0.299	

** Correlation is significant at the 0.01 level (2-tailed).
* Correlation is significant at the 0.05 level (2-tailed).
N=100 Soil sample

Table-4.34: Correlation table for Narmada District

Result and Discussion

4.2.3. Independent Sample Test (T-test) for both the Districts

Data obtained from both the districts were analyzed using an Independent sample T-test with the aid of the IBM SPSS statistics software package. For statistical analysis, datasets are prepared with variables of both the district. First, in the Independent sample T-test mean comparison have done because there is two independent variable (Mehsana and Narmada districts) as well as the significance of the data with sig. 2-tailed value or p-value. An Independent sample test has been done for both districts. There was a total of 200 samples were collected from both districts. So, the number of samples for a district was 100. In the Independent sample test, there were two sections. First, Group Statistics provides basic information about the group comparisons, like mean with mean standard error for soil parameter separately for both Mehsana and Narmada. The second section, Independent Samples Test, displays the results most relevant to the Independent Samples T-test. T-test for Equality of Means provides the results for the actual Independent Samples T-test and we focus on it. Note that t is calculated by dividing the mean difference by the standard error difference. The sign of the mean difference indicates the sign of the t- value. The positive t value indicates that the mean for the group is significantly greater than the mean for the other group the significant. If the p-value (sig. 2-tailed) is ≤ 0.05 then there is a significant difference in groups.

Group Statistics the Table-4.35 was showing: the mean moisture content of Mehsana was 14.0786 ± 0.797 %, pH was 7.8474 ±.0031, while moisture of Narmada was 28.3194 ± 0.667 %, pH was 6.6670 ± 0.041. The average EC and BD for Mehsana was 0.3476 ± 0.022 mmhos/cm and 1.3720 ± 0.008 g/cm^3 while 0.0939 ± 0.005 mmhos/cm EC and 1.4142 + 0.014 g/cm^3 BD for Narmada. Organic carbon and Nitrogen mean for Mehsana district soil was 0.4074 ± 0.020 % and 0.0351 ± 0.002 %, while OC 1.6080 ± 0.109 % and N 0.1386 ± 0.009 % was for Narmada. Moreover, the average Phosphorus was 5.5636 ± 0.196 ppm and Potassium was 121.2760 ± 5.594 ppm for Mehsana; while 4.2759 ± 0.197 ppm P and 82.4825 ± 6.196 ppm K for Narmada soil. For micronutrients, the mean Iron (Fe) of Mehsana soil was 7.7654 ± 0.201 ppm, Zink (Zn) was 0.5390 ± 0.030 ppm, Copper (Cu) was 0.7364 ± 0.030 ppm and Manganese (Mn) was 10.5159 ± 0.248 ppm. However, for

Result and Discussion

Narmada soil Fe was 13.8622 ± 0.220 ppm, Zn was 1.2080 ± 0.065 ppm, Cu was 0.8625 ± 0.042 ppm and Mn was 23.3474 ± 1.727 ppm. The mean Colony Forming Units (CFUs) per 0.1 gm for Mehsana soil was 1334518.02 ± 143488.915 while it was 1799751.40 ± 207995.804 for Narmada soil.

Soil Parameter	Group Statistics		Independent Samples Test	
			t-test for Equality of Means	
	District	Mean	t	Sig. (2-tailed)
Moisture (%)	Mehsana	14.0786 ± 0.797	-13.695	0.000
	Narmada	28.3194 ± 0.667	-13.695	0.000
pH	Mehsana	7.8474 ±.0031	22.890	0.000
	Narmada	6.6670 ± 0.041	22.890	0.000
EC(mmhos/cm)	Mehsana	0.3476 ± 0.022	10.743	0.000
	Narmada	0.0939 ± 0.005	10.743	0.000
BD (g/cm^3)	Mehsana	1.3720 ± 0.008	-2.453	0.015
	Narmada	1.4142 ± 0.014	-2.453	0.015
OC (%)	Mehsana	0.4074 ± 0.020	-10.748	0.000
	Narmada	1.6080 ± 0.109	-10.748	0.000
N (%)	Mehsana	0.0351 ± 0.002	-10.747	0.000
	Narmada	0.1386 ± 0.009	-10.747	0.000
P (ppm)	Mehsana	5.5636 ± 0.196	4.621	0.000
	Narmada	4.2759 ± 0.197	4.621	0.000
K (ppm)	Mehsana	121.2760 ± 5.594	4.647	0.000
	Narmada	82.4825 ± 6.196	4.647	0.000
Fe (ppm)	Mehsana	7.7654 ± 0.201	-20.421	0.000
	Narmada	13.8622 ± 0.220	-20.421	0.000
Zn (ppm)	Mehsana	0.5390 ± 0.030	-9.361	0.000
	Narmada	1.2080 ± 0.065	-9.361	0.000
Cu (ppm)	Mehsana	0.7364 ± 0.030	-2.420	0.016
	Narmada	0.8625 ± 0.042	-2.420	0.017
Mn (ppm)	Mehsana	10.5159 ± 0.248	-7.354	0.000
	Narmada	23.3474 ± 1.727	-7.354	0.000
CFUs	Mehsana	1334518.02 ± 143488.915	-1.841	0.067
	Narmada	1799751.40 ± 207995.804	-1.841	0.067

Table-4.35: Independent Sample Test (T-Test) for both the District

Based on the results of the Independent Samples Test, we can state the following:

There was a significant difference in the mean of all the soil parameters because p-values were smaller than 0.05 between Mehsana and Narmada district agriculture soil except Colony Forming Units.

Result and Discussion

4.3. Microbial Observations and Result

In the microbiological analysis, colony-forming units were counted for quantitative analysis for both districts. Quantitative analysis values have been added in the above data analysis part. In colonial morphology, types of growth of isolated bacteria on the solid media were recorded as colony characteristics. Furthermore, gram reaction, shapes, and arrangements of the organisms were interpreted by gram staining and motility test. Moreover, probable identifications of the bacterial isolates were noted with the Biochemical characterization.

4.3.1. Colonial Morphology of Bacterial Isolates

When attempting to identify unknown bacteria, it is important to note the cultural characteristics that the organisms exhibit in media. Proper isolation of individual species enables the examination of colonial shape and appearance, as well as other factors such as pigmentation, transparency, margin, texture, and smell. Gram reaction (Fig.-4.1, Fig.-4.2, and Fig.-4.3) and the possibility of motility were also checked. Cultural characteristics for NFB, PSB, and KSB are shown in Table-4.36.

Bacterial isolate	Colony shape	Cell shape & Arrangement	Colonial characteristics	Gram reaction	Motility
NFB Isolate	Circular	short rods single cell	white, unopaque, entire margin, and unsmooth	–	+
PSB Isolate	Circular	Rod single, in chain	white, translucent, entire margin, convex and smooth	+	+
KSB Isolate	Circular	short rods single cell	creamy, wet, smooth, and glassy luster pigment	–	–

Table-4.36: Cultural Characteristics of Bacterial Isolates

Above Table-4.36 shows that NFB and KSB isolates were gram-negative microorganisms but PSB was gram-positive. NFB and PSB isolates were motile while KSB isolate was non-motile. All three bacterial isolates were in a rod shape with single, in the chain, or cluster arrangements.

4.3.2. Biochemical Analysis/ Characterization of Bacterial Isolates

Biochemical analyses of unknown bacterial isolates were done for all three isolated organisms. In this characterization tests, results of sugar fermentation

Result and Discussion

tests, MR test, VP test, catalase test, oxidase test, nitrate tests, starch test, indole test, urea test, H_2S test, and citrate test were performed. Observations and reactions were noted and described below (Table-4.37) according to their biochemical discrimination, bacterial isolates were identified up to the genus level.

Identification parameter	Probable identification		
	NFB Isolate	*PSB Isolate*	*KSB Isolate*
Glucose	+	+	+
Lactose	−	D	A*
Mannitol	+*	+	+
MR	+	−	+
VP	+	+	−
Catalase	+	+	+
Oxidase	+	+	−
Nitrate	+*	+	−
Starch	NR	+	+*
Indole	+	−	−
Urea	−	D	−
H_2S	+	−	−
Citrate	NR	+	+*
Identification parameter	*Azatobacter sp.*	*Bacillus sp.*	*Bacillus sp.*
	Probable Identification		

Symbols: + 90 % or more strains positive; − 90 % or more strains negative; D different reaction in different taxa, * weak positive or negative; A (acid); G (gas), NR -no reaction observed

Table-4.37: Biochemical Characteristics of Bacterial Isolates

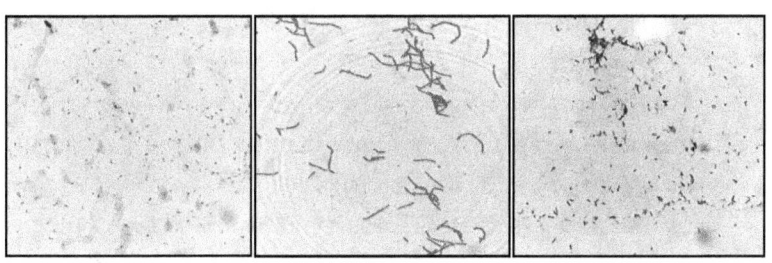

Fig.-4.1: Gram Negative NFB   Fig.-4.2: Gram Positive PSB   Fig.-4.3: Gram Negative KSB

Result and Discussion

4.4. Result of Molecular Study

In the Molecular study, two bacterial isolates were studied out of three isolates. One was the Nitrogen-fixing bacterial (NFB) isolate and the second Phosphate solubilizing bacterial (PSB) isolate. Potassium solubilizing bacterial (KSB) isolate was not studied. 16S rRNA partial sequence and Phylogenetic tree were analyzed for the NFB and PSB isolates. The sequence of the 16S rRNA gene has been widely used as a molecular clock to estimate relationships among bacteria (phylogeny), and has also become important as a tool to identify an unknown bacterium up to the genus or species level (Sacchi *et al.*, 2002). The sequence data for the 16S rRNA gene is highly conserved for different organisms and has also been shown to be very accurate for genus and species identification of Eubacteria. Carl Woese and colleagues used first of all the rRNA sequence data to examine evolutionary relationships among bacteria by comparing ribonuclease T1-generated oligonucleotides (Woese *et al.*, 1990). The 16S rRNA nucleotide sequences of the isolates were aligned with homologous regions from various actinomycetes, and the phylogenetic trees were constructed by the neighbor-joining method (Saitou and Nei, 1987).

4.4.1. 16S rRNA Partial Sequence Analysis of Strains DPN and DPP

Sequences of both the isolates were represented in Fig.-4.4 and Fig.-4.5. Comparison of the 16S rRNA partial sequences of strain DPN (Genbank accession number MT656171) with the GenBank database showed this isolate belongs to the Azotobacter genus, *Azotobacter* with > 99% certainty as perusing Basic Blast Tool of NCBI (Fig.-4.6 and Fig.-4.7). The strain is similar to several *Azotobacter* strains, such as *Azotobacter vinelandii* strain RFN32, *Azotobacter vinelandii* strain RFN04, *Azotobacter vinelandii* strain KGK3, and *Azotobacter vinelandii* strain ISSDS-436. The basic local elignment search tools from NCBI were used for BLAST and resulting 970 query length. Distribution of 100 blast hits on the query sequence was obtained as per Fig.-4.6 the total score up to 1750 from 1552 was found with 99 % of query coverage. 16S rRNA partial sequences of strain DPP (Genbank accession number MT656254) with the GenBank database showed this isolate belongs to the *Bacillus* genus, *Bacillus* with >99% certainty as perusing Basic Blast Tool of NCBI (Fig-4.8 and Fig-4.9). The strain is similar to several *Bacillus* strains, such as *Bacillus*

Result and Discussion

subtilis strain BJP-03, *Bacillus sp.* (in Bacteria) strain 6063, *Bacillus australimaris* strain KR4M-27, and *Bacillus sp.* MD-C14. The basic local elignment search tools from NCBI were used for BLAST and resulting 1171 query length. Distribution of 100 blast hits on the query sequence was obtained as per Fig.-4.8 the total score up to 2084 from 1965 was found with 99 % of query coverage.

```
AGCGGGACCTTCGGGTCGCCGGCGAGCGGCGGACGGGTGAGTAATGCCTAGGAATCTGCC
TGTTAGTGGGGGATAACTCGGGGAAACTCGCGCTAATACCGCATACGTCCTACGGGAGAA
AGTGGGGGACCCTCGGGCCTCACGCTAACAGATGAGCCTAGGTCGGATTAGCTAGTTGGT
GGGGTAAAGGCCCACCAAGGCGACGATCCGTAACTGGTCTGAGAGGATGATCAGTCACAC
TGGAACTGAGACACGGTCCAGGCTCCTACGGGAGGCAGCAGTGGGGAATATTGGACAATG
GGCGAAAGCCTGATCCAGCCATGCCGCGTGTGTGAAGAAGGTCTTCGGATTGTAAAGCAC
TTTAAGTTGGGAGGAAGGGCGCTCGGTGAATACCCAAGCCTCTTGACGTTACCGACAGAA
TAAGCACCGGCTAACTTCGTGCCAGCAGCCGCGGTAATACGAAGGGTGCAAGCGTTAATC
GGAATTACTGGGCGTAAAGCGCGCGTAGGTGGTTCGGCAAGTTGGATGTGAAAGCCCCGG
GCTCAACCTGGGAACCGCATCCAAAACTACTGGGCTAGAGTACGGTAGAGGGTGGTGGAA
TTTCCTGTGTAGCGGTGAAATGCGAAGATATAGGAAGGAACACCAGTGGCGAAGGCGACC
ACCTGGACCGATACTGACACTGAGGTGCGAAAGCGTGGGGAGCAAACAGGATTAGATACC
CTGGTAGTCCTTGCCGTAAACGATGTCGACTAGCCGTTGGGCTCCTTGAGAGCTTAGTGG
CGCAGCTAACGCATTAAGTCGACCGCCTGGGGAGTACGGCCGCAAGGTTAAAACTCAAAT
GAATTGACGGGGGCCCGCACAAGCGGTGGAGCATGTGGTTTAATTCGAAGCAACGCGAAG
AACCTTACCTGGCCTTGACATCCTGCGAACTTTCAAGGGATTGATTGGTGCCTTCGGGAA
CGCAGAGACA
```

Fig-4.4: Representation of sequenced *Azotobacter sp.* strain DPN
(GenBank Accession Number MT656171)

```
AGGGTTTGATCATGGCTCAGGACGAACGCTGGCGGCGTGCCTAATACATGCAAGTCGAGC
GGACAGAAGGGAGCTTGCTCCCGGATGTTAGCGGCGGACGGGTGAGTCACACGTGGGTAA
CCTGCCTGTAAGACTGGGATAACTCCGGGAAACCGGAGCTAATACCGGATAGTTCCTTGA
ACCGCATGGTTCCAGGATGAAAGACGGTTTCGGCTGTCACTTACAGATGGACCCGCGGCG
CATTAGCTAGTTGGTGAGGTACTGGCTCACCAAGGCGACGATGCGTAGCCGACCTGAGAG
GGTGATCGGCCACACTGGGACTGAGACACGGCCCAGACTCCTACGGGAGGCAGCAGTAGG
GAATCTTCCGCAATGGACGAAAGTCTGACGGAGCAAGGCCGCGTGAGTGAAGAAGGTTTT
CGGATCGTAAAGCTCTGTTGTTAGGGATGAACAAGTGCGAGAGTAACTGCTCGCACCTTG
ACGGTACCTAACCAGAAAGCCACGGCTAACTACGTGCCAGCAGCCGCGGTAATACGTAGG
TGGCAAGCGTTGTCCGGAATTATTGGGCGTAAAGGGCTCGCAGGCGGTTTCTTAAGTCTG
ATGGGAAATCCCCCGGCTCAACCGGGGGGGGTCATTGGAAACTGGGAAACTTGAGTGCAG
AAGAGGAGAGTGGAATTCCACGTGTAGCAGTGAAATGCGTAGAGATGTGGAGGAACACCA
GTGGCGAAGGCGACTCGCTGGTCTGTAACTGGCGAAAGCGTGGGGAGCGAACAGGATTAG
ATACCCTGGTAGTCCACGCCGTACACGATGAGTGCTAAGTGTTAGGGGGTTTCGCCCCTT
AGTGCTGCAGCTAACGCATTAAGCACTCCGCCTGGGGAGTACGATCGCAAGACTGAAACT
CAAATGAATTGACGGGGGCCCGCACAAGCGGTGGAGCATGTGTTTTAATTCGAAGCAACG
CGAAGAACCTTACCAGGTCTTGACATCCTCTGACAACCCTAGAGATAGGGCTTTCCCTTC
GGGGACAGAGTGACAGGTGGTGCATGGTTGTCGTCAGCTCGTGTCGAGAGATGTTGGGTT
AAGTCCCGCAACGAGCGCAACCCTTGATCTTAGTTGCCAGCATTCAGTTGGGCACTCTAA
GGTGACTGCCGGTGACAAACCGCAGGAAGGT
```

Fig-4.5: Representation of sequenced *Bacillus sp.* strain DPP
(GenBank Accession Number MT656254)

Page | 121

Result and Discussion

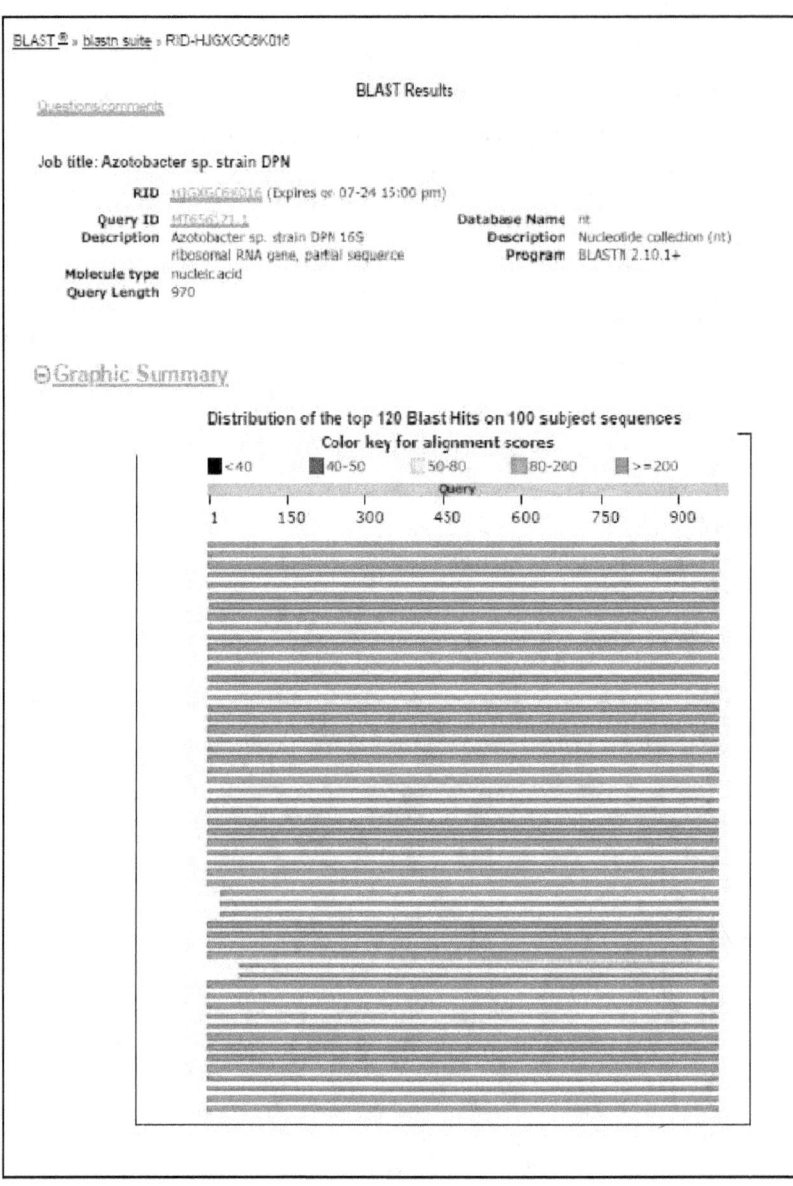

Fig-4.6: Output result of BLAST performed for *Azotobacter sp.* Strain DPN

Result and Discussion

Description	Max Score	Total Score	Query Cover	E value	Per. Ident	Accession
Azotobacter sp strain DPN 16S ribosomal RNA gene, partial sequence	1750	1750	100%	0.0	100.00%	gi|1868607125|MT656171.1
Azotobacter vinelandii strain RFN02 16S ribosomal RNA gene, partial sequence	1718	1718	100%	0.0	99.28%	gi|1150273963|KY731916.1
Azotobacter vinelandii strain RFN04 16S ribosomal RNA gene, partial sequence	1718	1718	100%	0.0	99.28%	gi|1150273963|KY731915.1
Azotobacter vinelandii strain KGK3 16S ribosomal RNA gene, partial sequence	1714	1714	100%	0.0	99.15%	gi|186241170|MT658715.1
Azotobacter vinelandii strain GGCS-406 16S ribosomal RNA gene, partial sequence	1714	1714	100%	0.0	99.15%	gi|1513083413|EF620452.1
Azotobacter vinelandii strain M-A 16S ribosomal RNA gene, partial sequence	1709	1709	100%	0.0	99.07%	gi|189625116|FJ032011.1
Uncultured bacterium clone N-05 16S ribosomal RNA gene, partial sequence	1708	1708	99%	0.0	99.07%	gi|007125729|HQ218443.1
Azotobacter vinelandii strain GGCS-423 16S ribosomal RNA gene, partial sequence	1706	1706	100%	0.0	99.07%	gi|1513033941|EF629445.1
Azotobacter vinelandii strain AV1 16S ribosomal RNA gene, partial sequence	1705	1705	100%	0.0	98.97%	gi|1625627306|MK847515.1
Azotobacter vinelandii strain 3-3 16S ribosomal RNA gene, partial sequence	1705	1705	100%	0.0	98.97%	gi|146156314|MH043585.1
Azotobacter sp strain G04 16S ribosomal RNA gene, partial sequence	1705	1705	100%	0.0	98.97%	gi|1315525741|MF431791.1
Azotobacter sp strain G02 16S ribosomal RNA gene, partial sequence	1705	1705	100%	0.0	98.97%	gi|1315525739|MF431789.1
Azotobacter sp strain G01 16S ribosomal RNA gene, partial sequence	1705	1705	100%	0.0	98.97%	gi|1315525738|MF431788.1
Azotobacter sp strain N2106 16S ribosomal RNA gene, partial sequence	1705	1705	100%	0.0	98.97%	gi|1315525737|MF431787.1
Azotobacter vinelandii CA6, complete genome	1705	10232	100%	0.0	98.97%	gi|482534342|CP005095.1
Azotobacter vinelandii CA, complete genome	1705	10232	100%	0.0	98.97%	gi|482532343|CP005094.1
Azotobacter vinelandii strain VBRD 102612 16S ribosomal RNA partial sequence	1705	1705	100%	0.0	98.97%	gi|621252638|NR_114155.1

Fig-4.7: Output result of BLAST performed for *Azotobacter sp.* Strain DPN (page-1)

Page | 123

Result and Discussion

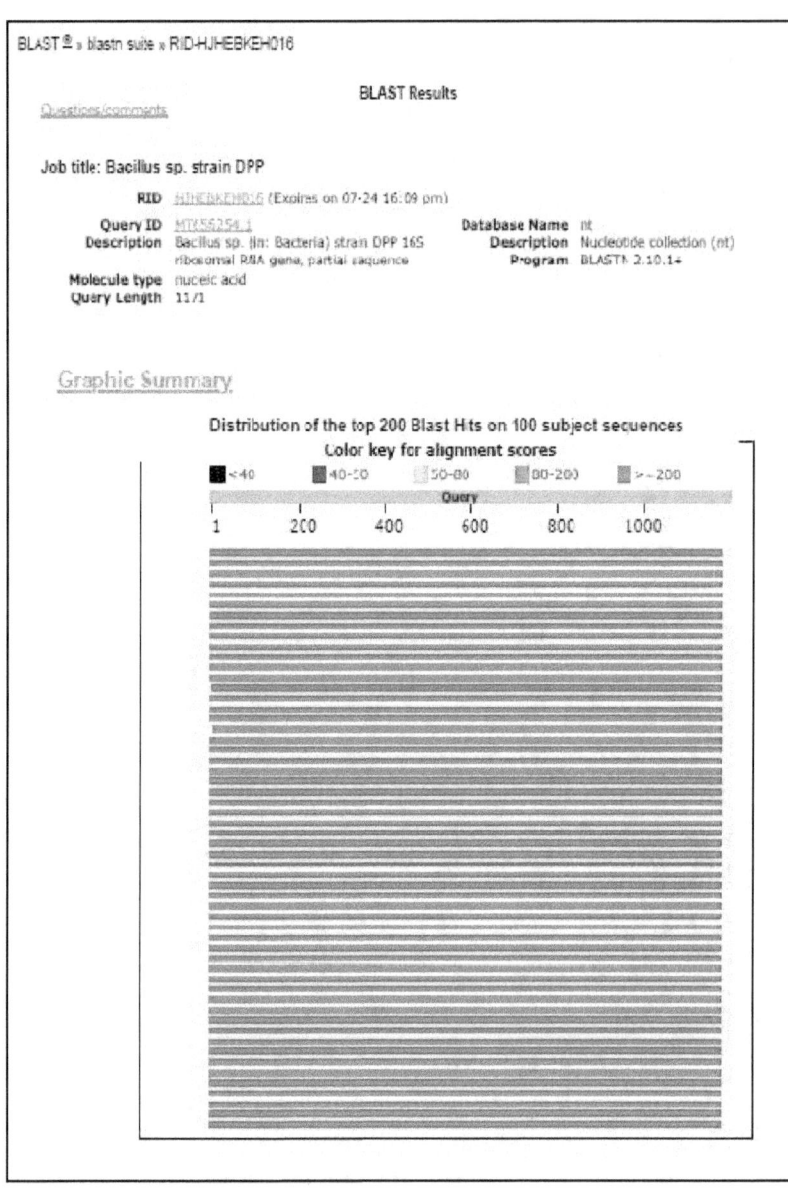

Fig-4.8: Output result of BLAST performed for *Bacillus sp.* Strain DPP

Result and Discussion

Descriptions

Sequences producing significant alignments:

Description	Max Score	Total Score	Query Cover	E value	Per. ident	Accession
Bacillus sp. (in Bacteria) strain DPP 16S ribosomal RNA gene, partial sequence	2084	2084	100%	0.0	100.00%	gi1860007529 MT654254.1
Bacillus subtilis strain EJP-03 16S ribosomal RNA gene, partial sequence	2012	2012	100%	0.0	98.53%	gi1872708385 KU936341.1
Bacillus sp. (in Bacteria) strain 6053 16S ribosomal RNA gene, partial sequence	1974	1974	100%	0.0	97.46%	gi1635309068 MT305628.1
Bacillus australimaris strain KR4M-27 16S ribosomal RNA gene, partial sequence	1974	1974	100%	0.0	97.46%	gi1779791419 MN762434.1
Bacillus sp. MD-C14 16S ribosomal RNA gene, partial sequence	1974	1974	100%	0.0	97.46%	gi874527183 KP287235.1
Bacillus sp. MD-A10 16S ribosomal RNA gene, partial sequence	1974	1974	100%	0.0	97.46%	gi874527168 KP207205.1
Bacillus sp. SAP751.1 16S ribosomal RNA gene, partial sequence	1974	1974	100%	0.0	97.46%	gi329764212 JX057873.1
Uncultured Bacillus sp. clone KVGNJ5 16S ribosomal RNA gene, partial sequence	1974	1974	100%	0.0	97.46%	gi210075770 EU780453.1
Bacillus sp. G1DM-4 16S ribosomal RNA gene, partial sequence	1974	1974	100%	0.0	97.46%	gi89474134 DQ415781.1
Bacillus pumilus isolate ZB13 16S ribosomal RNA gene, partial sequence	1974	1974	100%	0.0	97.46%	gi1443608314 EF491524.1
Bacillus pumilus strain rg2-s2 16S ribosomal RNA gene, partial sequence	1974	1974	100%	0.0	97.46%	gi79757624 DQ299295.1
Bacillus pumilus strain NRC21 16S ribosomal RNA gene, partial sequence	1971	1971	100%	0.0	97.38%	gi672105418 KJ817373.1
Bacterium Te56R 16S ribosomal RNA gene, partial sequence	1971	1971	100%	0.0	97.38%	gi665050201 AT587832.1
Bacillus sp. MF 16S ribosomal RNA gene, partial sequence	1970	1970	99%	0.0	97.46%	gi1028910473 KU925494.1
Bacillus australimaris strain GIM-E3 16S ribosomal RNA gene, partial sequence	1969	1969	100%	0.0	97.38%	gi1851755650 MT501005.1
Bacillus safensis strain FgKB20 chromosome, complete genome	1969	15676	100%	0.0	97.38%	gi1733380297 CP043404.1
Bacillus safensis strain sami chromosome	1969	1969	100%	0.0	97.38%	gi1491745074 CP692610.1
Bacillus sp. (in Bacteria) strain Lewis_Bac_16 16S ribosomal RNA gene, partial sequence	1969	1969	99%	0.0	97.54%	gi1571079010 MN133254.1

Fig-4.9: Output result of BLAST performed for *Bacillus sp.* Strain DPP (page-1)

Result and Discussion

```
GenBank

Azotobacter sp. strain DPN 16S ribosomal RNA gene, partial sequence
GenBank: MT656171.1
FASTA  Graphics
LOCUS       MT656171               970 bp    DNA     linear   BCT 21-JUL-2020
DEFINITION  Azotobacter sp. strain DPN 16S ribosomal RNA gene, partial
            sequence.
ACCESSION   MT656171
VERSION     MT656171.1
KEYWORDS    .
SOURCE      Azotobacter sp.
  ORGANISM  Azotobacter sp.
            Bacteria; Proteobacteria; Gammaproteobacteria; Pseudomonadales;
            Pseudomonadaceae; Azotobacter; unclassified Azotobacter.
REFERENCE   1  (bases 1 to 970)
  AUTHORS   Prajapati,D.N. and George,L.B.
  TITLE     Direct Submission
  JOURNAL   Submitted (23-JUN-2020) Life Sciences Department, Gujarat
            University, University School of Sciences, Gujarat University,
            Navrangpura, Ahmedabad, Gujarat 380009, India
COMMENT     ##Assembly-Data-START##
            Sequencing Technology :: Sanger dideoxy sequencing
            ##Assembly-Data-END##
FEATURES             Location/Qualifiers
     source          1..970
                     /organism="Azotobacter sp."
                     /mol_type="genomic DNA"
                     /strain="DPN"
                     /isolation_source="rhizospheric soil"
                     /host="Agricultural farm"
                     /db_xref="taxon:1872672"
                     /country="India"
                     /identified_by="Dipakkumar Natvarbhai Prajapati"
     rRNA            <1..>970
                     /product="16S ribosomal RNA"
ORIGIN
        1 agcgggacct tcgggtcgcc ggcgagcggc ggacgggtga gtaatgccta ggaatctgcc
       61 tgttagtggg ggataactcg gggaaactcg cgctaatacc gcatacgtcc tacgggagaa
      121 agtggggggac cctcgggcct cacgctaasca gatgagccta ggtcggatta gctagttggt
      181 ggggtaaagg cccaccaagg cgacgatccg taactggtct gagaggatga tcagtcacac
      241 tgggactgag acacggccca gactcctacg ggaggcagca gtgggggata tgggcaatg
      301 ggcgaaagcc tgatccagcc atgccgcgtg tgtgaagaag gtcttcggat tgtaaagcac
      361 tttaagttgg gaggaagggc gctcggtgaa tcccaagcc tcttgacgtt accgacagaa
      421 taagcaccgg ctaacttcgt gccagcagcc gcggtaatac gaagggtgca agcgttaatc
      481 ggaattactg gcgtaaagc gcgcgtaggt ggttggcgaa gttggatgtg aaagcccgg
      541 gctcaacctg ggaaccgcat ccaaaactac tgggctagag tacggtagag ggtggtggaa
      601 tttcctgtgt agcggtgaaa tgcgaagata tggaaggaa caccagtggc gaaggcgacc
      661 acctggaccg atactgacac tgaggtgcga aegcgtgggg agcaaacagg attagatacc
      721 ctggtagtcc ttgccgtaaa cgatgtcgac tagccgttgg gctccttgag agcttagtgg
      781 cgcagctaac gcattaagtc gaccgcctgg ggagtacggc cgcaaggtta aaactcaaat
      841 gaattgacgg gggcccgcac aagcggtgga gcatgtggtt taattcgaag caacgcgaag
      901 aaccttacct ggccttgaca tcctgcgaac tttcaaggga ttgattggtg ccttcgggaa
      961 cgcagagaca
//
```

Fig.-4.10: GeneBank entry of *Azotobacter sp.* Strain DPN

The sequence of Strain DPN was submitted to National Centre for Biological Information (NCBI). They registered it with the accession number MT656171. The details of the sequence at NCBI are given in Fig.-4.10. The G+C content was 55.57%.

Result and Discussion

```
GenBank

Bacillus sp. (in: Bacteria) strain DPP 16S ribosomal RNA gene, partial sequence
GenBank: MT656254.1
FASTA  Graphics

Go to: ∨

LOCUS       MT656254                1171 bp    DNA     linear   BCT 21-JUL-2020
DEFINITION  Bacillus sp. (in: Bacteria) strain DPP 16S ribosomal RNA gene,
            partial sequence.
ACCESSION   MT656254
VERSION     MT656254.1
KEYWORDS    .
SOURCE      Bacillus sp. (in: Bacteria)
  ORGANISM  Bacillus sp. (in: Bacteria)
            Bacteria; Firmicutes; Bacilli; Bacillales; Bacillaceae; Bacillus.
REFERENCE   1  (bases 1 to 1171)
  AUTHORS   Prajapati,D.N. and George,L.B.
  TITLE     Direct Submission
  JOURNAL   Submitted (23-JUN-2020) Life Sciences Department, Gujarat
            University, University School of Sciences, Gujarat University,
            Navrangpura, Ahmedabad, Gujarat 380009, India
COMMENT     ##Assembly-Data-START##
            Sequencing Technology :: Sanger dideoxy sequencing
            ##Assembly-Data-END##
FEATURES             Location/Qualifiers
     source          1..1171
                     /organism="Bacillus sp. (in: Bacteria)"
                     /mol_type="genomic DNA"
                     /strain="DPP"
                     /isolation_source="Rhizosperic soil"
                     /host="Agricultural farm"
                     /db_xref="taxon:1409"
                     /country="India"
                     /identified_by="Dipakkumar Natvarbhai Prajapati"
     rRNA            <1..>1171
                     /product="16S ribosomal RNA"
ORIGIN
        1 agggtttgat categctcag gacgaacgct ggcggcgtgc ctaatacatg caagtcgagc
       61 ggacagaagg gagcttgctc ccggatgtta gcggcggacg ggtgagtcac acgtgggtaa
      121 cctgcctgta agactgggat aactccggga aaccggagct aataccggat agttccttga
      181 accgcatggt tccaggatga aagacggttt cggctgtcac ttacagatgg accgcggcg
      241 cattagctag ttggtgaggt aactggctcac caaggcgacg atgcgtagcc gacctgagag
      301 ggtgatcggc cacactggga ctgagacacg gcccagactc ctacgggagg cagcagtagg
      361 gaatcttccg caatgcacga aagtctgacg gagcaaggcc gcgtgagtga agaaggtttt
      421 cggatcgtaa agctctgttg ttagggatga acaagtccga gagtaactgc tcgcacccttg
      481 acggtaccta accagaaagc cacggctaac tacgtgccag cagccgcggt aatacgtagg
      541 tggcaagcgt tgtccggaat tattgggcgt aaagggctcg caggcggttt cttaagtctg
      601 atggaaaatc ccccggctca accgggggg gtcattggaa actgggaaac ttgagtgcag
      661 aagaggagag tggaattcca cgtgtagcag tgaaatgcgt agagatgtgg aggaacacca
      721 gtggcgaagg cgactcgctg gtcgtgtaact ggcaaaagcg tgggagcga acaggattag
      781 ataccctggt agtccacgcc gtacacgatg agtgctaagt gttgggggt ttcgcccctt
      841 agtgctgcag ctaacgcatt aagcactccg cctgggggat acgatcgcaa gactgaaact
      901 caaatgaatt gacggggcc gcacaagcgg tggagcatg tgttttaatt cgaagcaacg
      961 cgaagaacct taccaggtct tgacatcctc tgacaacct agagataggg ctttcccttc
     1021 gggacagag tgacaggtgg tgcatggttg tcgtcagctc gtgtcgagag atgttgggtt
     1081 aagtcccgca acgagcgcaa cccttgatct tagttgccag cattcagttg ggcactctaa
     1141 ggtgactgcc ggtgacaaac cgcaggaagg t
//
```

Fig-4.11: GeneBank entry of *Bacillus sp.* Strain DPP

The sequence of Strain DPP was submitted to National Centre for Biological Information (NCBI). They registered it with the accession number MT656254. The details of the sequence at NCBI are given in Fig.-4.11. The G+C content was 55.25%.

Result and Discussion

4.4.2. Phylogenetic Analysis of Strains DPN and DPP

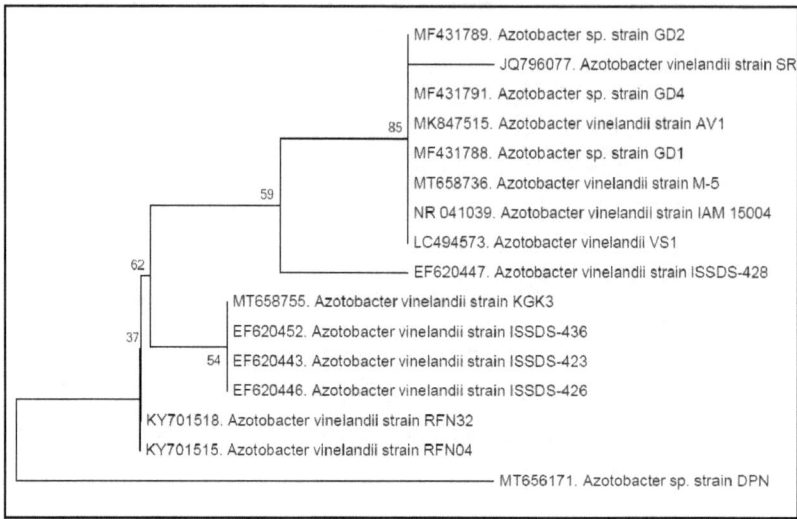

Fig-4.12: Phylogenetic Tree Representing the Position of *Azotobacter sp.* Strain DPN

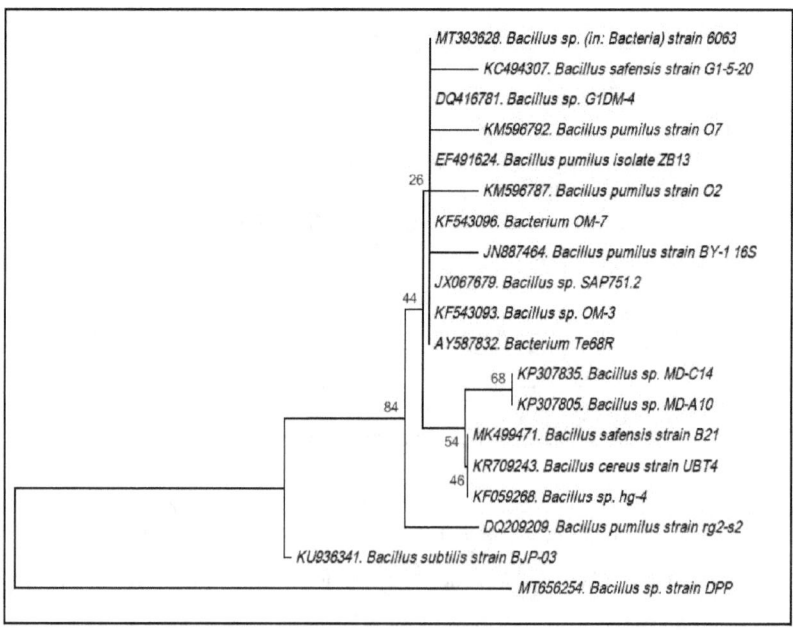

Fig-4.13: Phylogenetic Tree Representing the Position of *Bacillus sp.* Strain DPP

Result and Discussion

A comparison of the 16S rRNA gene sequences with the non-redundant collection (NCBI GenBank) of sequences was performed using BLAST (Zhang et al., 2000). Several sequences of the genus *Azotobacter* and *Bacillus* were aligned with the 16S rRNA gene sequences with greater than 90% sequence similarity. Further, the phylogenetic tree derived from the neighbor-joining analysis showed a correlation between the 16S rDNA sequence of the DPN strain and other *Azotobacter* strains in the NCBI database. That close relationship is shown in Fig.-4.12. Neighbor-joining analysis for the DPP strain and other *Bacillus* strains is shown in Fig.-4.13. The creation of a phylogenetic tree supported on the 16S rRNA gene helps to locate the isolate in its preferred taxa. On the other hand high sequence similarity and close evolutionary distance showed in the derived phylogenetic tree among the 16S rRNA gene sequence suggest that isolated strain might be involved parallel to a phylogenetic tree was built allowing for similar sequences of BLAST results for studying the evolutionary relationship of *Azotobacter sp.* strain DPN and *Bacillus sp.* strain DPP with closely related *Azotobacter sp.* and *Bacillus sp.* The number of copies of rRNA genes also varies in different microorganisms. Intragenomic heterogeneity is also observed in the sequences of organisms having a high copy number of genes. The phylogenetic analysis is done based on matching the 16S rRNA sequence but the isolates which are shown closely related here can also differ to varying degrees. The number of copies reflects on the ecological background and adaptability of the particular organism (Coenye and Vandamme, 2003).

4.5. Soil Amendment and Bio-rejuvenation Result

4.5.1. Primary Soil Analyzed Result of the Selected Fields

Agricultural sample number 1 site and agricultural sample number 68 site were selected for the Mehsana district field 1 and Mehsana district field 2. While from the Dediyapada taluka of Narmada district, agricultural sample number 38 site was selected for Narmada field. Table-4.38 shows primary soil analyzed results of the selected agricultural fields which were selected for the amendment and bio-rejuvenation studies.

Result and Discussion

➡ Selected Fields ⬇ Soil parameters	Mehsana field 1	Mehsana field 2	Narmada field
Moisture (%)	7.76	24.69	21.20
pH	7.45	7.95	6.41
EC (mmhos/cm)	0.18	0.34	0.07
BD (g/cm^3)	1.32	1.36	1.21
OC (%)	0.38	0.48	1.84
N (%)	0.03	0.04	0.16
P (ppm)	7.70	4.82	3.09
K (ppm)	55.06	130.58	64.58
Fe (ppm)	5.60	5.00	15.78
Zn (ppm)	0.80	0.82	2.01
Cu (ppm)	0.36	0.92	0.45
Mn (ppm)	13.30	10.60	14.22

Table-4.38: Soil Analyses of the Selected Agricultural Fields

4.5.2. Soil Analyzed Result after the Amendment of Bacterial Isolates

➡ Fields & days ⬇ Soil parameters	Mehsana field 1			Mehsana field 2			Narmada field		
	3 days	10 days	25 days	3 days	10 days	25 days	3 days	10 days	25 days
Moisture (%)	12.76	8.20	16.49	26.86	28.78	22.53	24.20	25.32	25.99
pH	7.55	7.38	7.28	7.75	7.39	7.23	7.46	7.02	7.16
EC (mmhos/cm)	0.24	0.20	0.22	0.36	0.34	0.34	0.14	0.14	0.18
BD (g/cm^3)	1.31	1.29	1.26	1.36	1.35	1.31	1.21	1.26	1.26
OC (%)	2.29	1.72	1.05	1.68	1.44	1.20	2.74	2.50	2.45
N (%)	0.07	0.12	0.18	0.05	0.06	0.10	0.17	0.18	0.18
P (ppm)	7.76	7.92	8.89	4.88	5.69	6.38	3.29	3.72	4.99
K (ppm)	56.05	58.70	62.50	131.05	134.32	141.40	65.80	66.26	72.82
Fe (ppm)	5.52	5.39	5.74	5.72	5.95	5.78	15.80	15.70	15.84
Zn (ppm)	0.80	0.82	0.83	0.82	0.81	0.86	2.00	2.12	2.06
Cu (ppm)	0.35	0.40	0.38	0.94	0.90	0.86	0.45	0.40	0.42
Mn (ppm)	13.26	13.00	13.54	10.86	10.98	11.02	14.10	14.30	14.28

Table-4.39: Soil Analyzed Result after the Amendment of Bacterial Isolates

In the amendment study, all the three soil N, P, and K nutrient enhancing microorganisms with suitable carriers (Fig.-4.14) were applied in the fields (Fig.-4.15, Fig.-4.16, Fig.-4.17, and Fig.-4.18). After the amendments, soil nutrient quality was increased in both the district fields were shown in soil analysis (Table-4.39).

Result and Discussion

Fig.-4.14: Bacterial Isolates Mixed with Carrier for Amendment

Fig.-4.15: Castor field 1 Mehsana District Fig.-4.16: Castor field 2 Mehsana District

Fig.-4.17: Sugarcane field Narmada District Fig.-4.18: Sugarcane field Narmada District

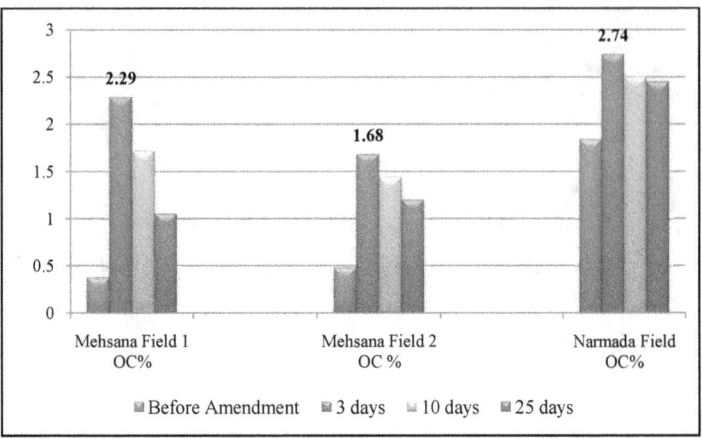

Graph-4.29: Comparison of OC% in Selected Fields after Amendment

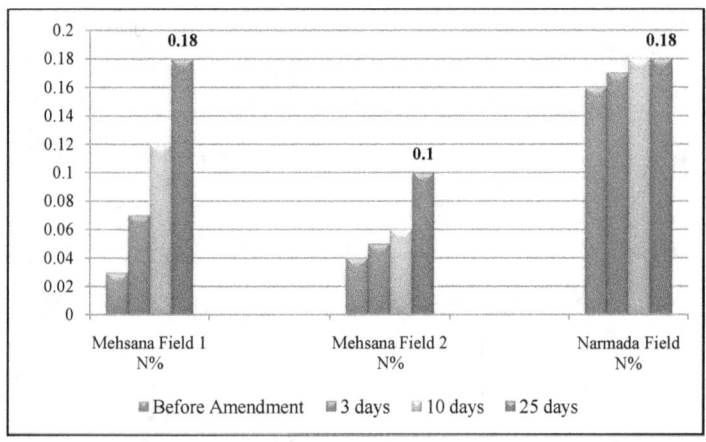

Graph-4.30: Comparison of N% in Selected Fields after Amendment

Soil organic carbon content in the fields was suddenly increased after the amendment and then gradually decreased. This was due to the carrier which was applied along with bacteria (Graph-4.29). After the amendment, the Nitrogen percentage of the fields was continuously rising till the last soil analysis (Graph-4.30).

Result and Discussion

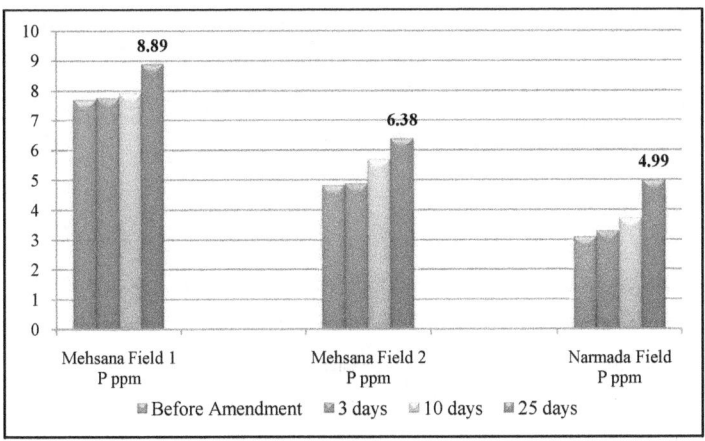

Graph-4.31: Comparison of P (ppm) in Selected Fields after Amendment

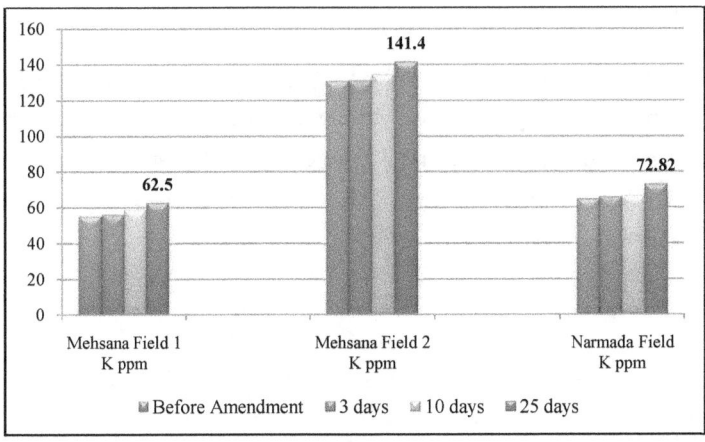

Graph-4.32: Comparison of K (ppm) in Selected Fields after Amendment

After the amendment of isolated bacteria in both the district soil, Phosphorous (Graph-31) and Potassium (Graph-32) values were gradually increased.

Result and Discussion

4.5.3. Result of the Crop Growth and Productivity

Character	Mehsana field 1 & 2 (Castor plant)		Narmada field (Sugarcane plant)	
	Normal	After Amendment	Normal	After Amendment
Plant height (cm)	195	258	171	214
Plant dry weight (g)	960	1350	1740	2030
No. of branches (nos)	14 main + other sub branches	28 main + other sub branches	Cluster of 5	Cluster of 9
Root length (cm)	67	98	12	21

Table-4.40: Effect of Amendment on Crop fields of both the Districts

After the treatment of soil nutrient enhancing microorganisms, soil fertility was reported to increase. Soil amendment was done for the Mehsana district castor agriculture fields and the Narmada district sugarcane agriculture land. The effect of the isolated soil microbes treatment was reported as significant. Nitrogen-fixing Azotobacter sp. strain DPN, Phosphate solubilizing Bacillus sp. strain DPP and Potassium Solubilizing Bacillus sp. were applied in the fields and responded positively for the plant growth.

In Table-4.40, the comparison is shown between normal plant and treatment given plants of castor and sugarcane. The plant average height, dry weight, number of branches, and root length were greater than the normal plant in both the crop fields. Yields of both the crop were responded positively with the application of microorganism culture, maybe due to the complementary effect of nutrient enhancing microbes on chemical fertilizers (Hema *et al.*, 2004).

www.ingramcontent.com/pod-product-compliance
Lightning Source LLC
LaVergne TN
LVHW010226070526
838199LV00062B/4730